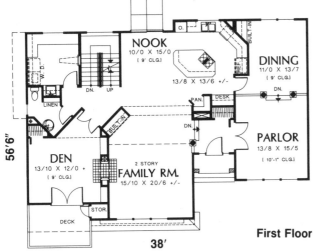

First Floor

56'6"

38'

3 CAR GARAGE UNDER

NOOK 10/0 X 15/0 (9' CLG.)

DINING 11/0 X 13/7 (9' CLG.)

13/8 X 13/6 +/-

PARLOR 13/8 X 15/5 (10'-1" CLG.)

DESK

PAN.

LINEN

DEN 13/10 X 12/0 + (9' CLG.)

2 STORY FAMILY RM. 15/10 X 20/6 +/-

STOR.

DECK

W. D.

DN. UP

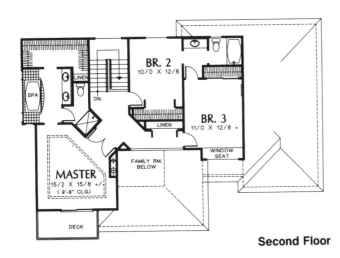

Second Floor

SPA

LINEN

BR. 2 10/0 X 12/8

BR. 3 11/0 X 12/8

LINEN

DN.

WINDOW SEAT

MASTER 15/2 X 15/8 +/- (9'-9" CLG.)

FAMILY RM. BELOW

DECK

Hillside Home Has Great Street Appeal

Secluded Master Suite Promises Privacy

First floor—1713 sq. ft.
Second floor—998 sq. ft.
Lower level—102 sq. ft.
Total living space—2813 sq. ft.
3-4 bedrooms, 2½ baths
Shown with a basement

- Plan is designed for lots that slope approximately 8' in depth.

- The den can be converted to the fourth bedroom and shares an open fireplace in the family room.

- The master suite includes a spa tub with separate shower, walk-in closet and double-bowled vanity.

- The secondary bedrooms have separate entrances to the bathroom and plenty of closet space.

Plan number AMA-2402-DF93. See index for pricing details. Plan by Alan Mascord Design Associates.

The diagrams presented here constitute only floor plans and elevations. Purchasers are advised to consult their state and local building regulations and a state-certified architect prior to any construction related to these plans.

Rear Elevation

Turned Garage Adds Street Appeal

First floor—1944 sq. ft.
Second floor—954 sq. ft.
Total living space—2898 sq. ft.
4 bedrooms, 3½ baths
Shown with a basement

- ✔ A formal gallery separates the dining room from the great room.

- ✔ Stairs to the second floor are conveniently located between the great room and breakfast room.

- ✔ Island kitchen includes large pantry cupboard. Laundry room is nearby.

- ✔ First-floor master suite is very private.

- ✔ Study and great room each have a fireplace.

Plan number DTA-L2610-DT91. See index for pricing details. Plan by Design Traditions.

The diagrams presented here constitute only floor plans and elevations. Purchasers are advised to consult their state and local building regulations and a state-certified architect prior to any construction related to these plans.

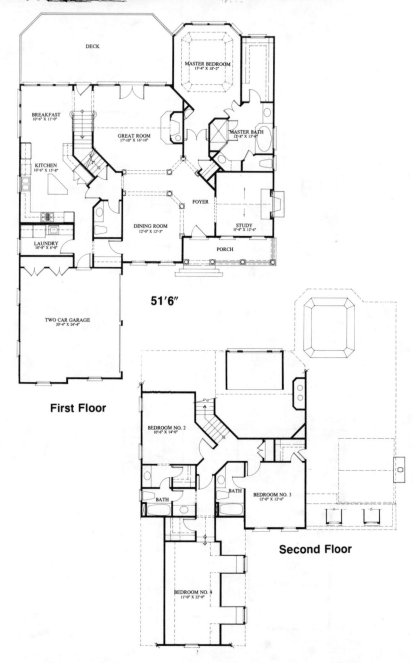

First Floor

Second Floor

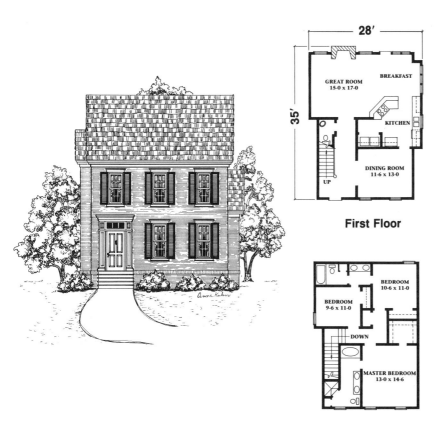

First Floor

28'

35'

GREAT ROOM
15-0 x 17-0

BREAKFAST

KITCHEN

DINING ROOM
11-6 x 13-0

UP

BEDROOM
10-6 x 11-0

BEDROOM
9-6 x 11-0

DOWN

MASTER BEDROOM
13-0 x 14-6

Second Floor

This Two-Story Classic Is Perfect For First-Time Buyers

First floor—914 sq. ft.
Second floor—823 sq. ft.
Total living space—1737 sq. ft.
3 bedrooms, 2½ baths
Shown with a concrete slab

✔ Master bedroom has a walk-in closet.

✔ Bedrooms two and three share a full bath complete with dual vanities.

✔ Kitchen is designed to function efficiently to the great room and breakfast area.

Plan number HR-623-9207. See index for pricing details. Plan by Historical Replications Inc.

The diagrams presented here constitute only floor plans and elevations. Purchasers are advised to consult their state and local building regulations and a state-certified architect prior to any construction related to these plans.

High Impact Ceilings Give Expandable Home Added Impact

Main floor—1321 sq. ft.
Lower floor—591 sq. ft.
Total living space—1912 sq. ft.
3 bedrooms, 2 baths
Shown with a basement

✔ Striking vaulted ceiling highlights the living room.

✔ Fireplace serves as an appealing gathering spot.

✔ Breakfast nook is highlighted by a bay window and a custom ceiling treatment.

✔ Private bath and walk-in closet are special features of the master suite.

✔ Secondary bedrooms also have sloped ceilings.

Plan number TGC-595-SU93. See index for price details. Plan by The Garlinghouse Co.

The diagrams presented here constitute only floor plans and elevations. Purchasers are advised to consult their state and local building regulations and a state-certified architect prior to any construction related to these plans.

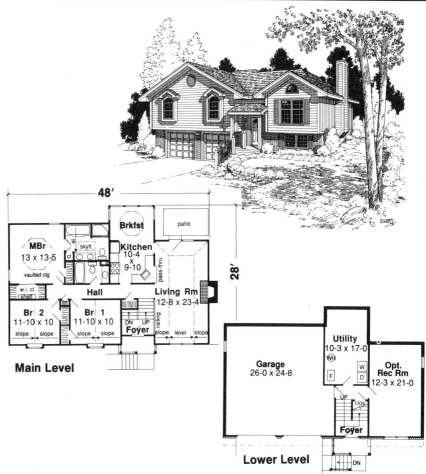

48'

MBr
13 x 13-5
vaulted clg

w.i. cl
shelf

Brkfst

patio

Kitchen
10-4
x
9-10

pass-thru

Hall

Living Rm
12-8 x 23-4

28'

Br 2
11-10 x 10
slope   slope

Br 1
11-10 x 10
slope   slope

DN   UP
railing

Foyer
slope   level   slope

Main Level

Garage
26-0 x 24-8

Utility
10-3 x 17-0
WH
F

W
D

Opt.
Rec Rm
12-3 x 21-0

UP

clos

Foyer

DN

Lower Level

Attractive Corner Fireplace Sparks Living Room

**First floor—1603 sq. ft.
Second floor—544 sq. ft.
Finished basement space—238 sq. ft.
Total living space—2385 sq. ft.
3-4 bedrooms, 2½ baths
Shown with a basement**

✔ Very private master suite occupies the entire second floor.

✔ Wet bar serves the entertainment areas.

✔ Sunny breakfast area adjoins the kitchen.

✔ Secondary bedrooms each have access to a deck.

✔ The master bedroom is on its own level for added privacy. It features a large walk-in closet and deluxe bath.

Plan number QJA-1991-SU93. See index for price details. Plan by Quincy Johnson & Associates.

The diagrams presented here constitute only floor plans and elevations. Purchasers are advised to consult their state and local building regulations and a state-certified architect prior to any construction related to these plans.

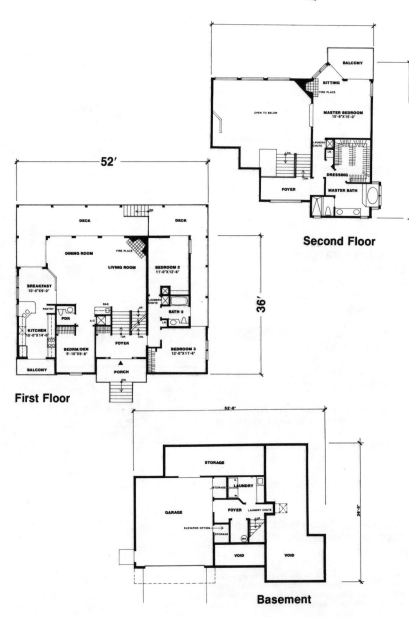

Second Floor

First Floor

Basement

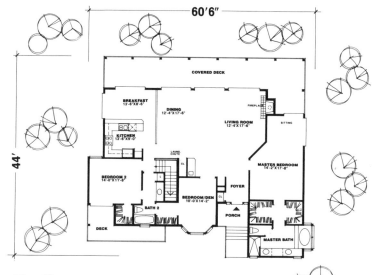

First Floor

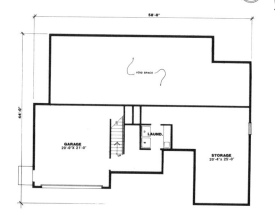

Basement

Bedroom/Den Is Planned For Versatility

Main floor—2109 sq. ft.
Finished basement space—195 sq. ft.
Total living space—2304 sq. ft.
2-3 bedrooms, 2 baths
Shown with a basement

- Foyer includes a handy coat closet.

- Den/bedroom includes a bay window, closet space and private access to the main bath.

- Minimal use of walls lets living, dining room space flow together.

- Breakfast area adjoins kitchen over a snack bar counter.

- Private sitting area is included in the master suite.

Plan number QJA-1989-SU93. See index for price details. Plan by Quincy Johnson & Associates.

The diagrams presented here constitute only floor plans and elevations. Purchasers are advised to consult their state and local building regulations and a state-certified architect prior to any construction related to these plans.

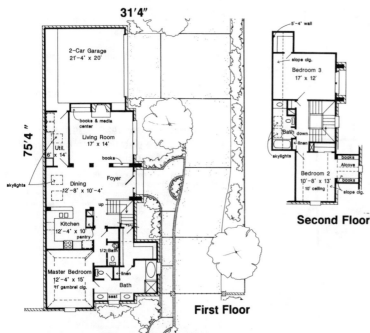

31'4"

75'4"

2-Car Garage
21'-4" x 20'

books & media center

Living Room
17' x 14'

Util.
6' x 14'

books

Dining
12'-8" x 10'-4'

Foyer

skylights

up

Kitchen
12'-4" x 10'

pantry

1/2 Bath

Master Bedroom
12'-4" x 15'
11' gambrel clg.

linen

Bath

seat

First Floor

5'-4" wall

slope clg.

Bedroom 3
17' x 12'

Bath

down

linen

skylights

books

Alcove

Bedroom 2
10'-8" x 13'
10' ceiling

books

slope clg.

Second Floor

Skylights Ensure Bright, Cheerful Interior

**First floor—1401 sq. ft.
Second floor—578 sq. ft.
Total living space—1979 sq. ft.
3 bedrooms, 2½ baths
Shown with a concrete slab**

✔ First-class master suite is designed to pamper with its spacious bath.

✔ Kitchen features a pass-through to the dining area.

✔ Living room features a fireplace and built-in bookshelves.

Plan number LWG-1091-SU93. See index for price details. Plan by Larry W. Garnett & Associates Inc.

The diagrams presented here constitute only floor plans and elevations. Purchasers are advised to consult their state and local building regulations and a state-certified architect prior to any construction related to these plans.

Living, Dining Rooms Share View To Increase Sense Of Space

**Total living space—1530 sq. ft.
2 bedrooms, 2 baths
Shown with a concrete slab foundation**

✔ Triple skylights and built-in bookshelves highlight the private study.

✔ Master suite includes a walk-in closet and separate bath.

✔ Living room features a fireplace framed by windows.

Plan number LWG-1090-SU93. See index for price details. Plan by Larry W. Garnett & Associates Inc.

The diagrams presented here constitute only floor plans and elevations. Purchasers are advised to consult their state and local building regulations and a state-certified architect prior to any construction related to these plans.

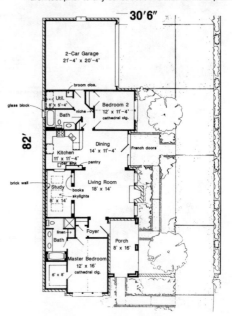

30'6"

82'

2-Car Garage
21'-4" x 20'-4"

broom clos.

Util.
8' x 5'-4"

glass block

niche

Bath

Bedroom 2
12' x 11'-4"
cathedral clg.

Kitchen
11' x 11'-4"

Dining
14' x 11'-4"

French doors

pantry

brick wall

Study
8' x 14'

books

Living Room
18' x 14'

skylights

linen

Foyer

Bath

Porch
8' x 16'

Master Bedroom
12' x 16'
cathedral clg.

6' x 8'

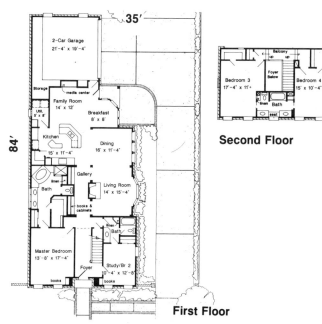

35'

2-Car Garage
21'-4" x 19'-4"

Storage

media center

Family Room
14' x 12'

Util.
5' x 5'

Breakfast
8' x 8'

Kitchen
15' x 11'-4"

Dining
16' x 11'-4"

linen

Gallery

Bath

Living Room
14' x 15'-4"

books & cabinets

linen

Bath

Master Bedroom
13'-8" x 17'-4"

Study/Br 2
10'-4" x 12'-8"

Foyer

books

books

84'

First Floor

Balcony
up   up

Bedroom 3
17'-4" x 11'

Foyer
Below

Bedroom 4
15' x 10'-4"

linen   Bath

seat

Second Floor

Extra Bedroom Offers Study Option

First floor—1947 sq. ft.
Second floor—695 sq. ft.
Total living space—2642 sq. ft.
3-4 bedrooms, 3 baths
Shown with a concrete slab

✔ Family room combines space with the kitchen, breakfast area creating a spacious informal zone.

✔ Study/bedroom has private access to a full bath.

✔ Walk-in closets are included in each of the other bedrooms.

Plan number LWG-1089-SU93. See index for price details. Plan by Larry W. Garnett & Associates Inc.

The diagrams presented here constitute only floor plans and elevations. Purchasers are advised to consult their state and local building regulations and a state-certified architect prior to any construction related to these plans.

Built-In Media Center Highlights Family Room

First floor—1973 sq. ft.
Second floor—344 sq. ft.
Total living space—2317 sq. ft.
2-3 bedrooms, 3 baths
Shown with a concrete slab

✔ Open kitchen features a corner pantry and a pass-through counter to the family zone.

✔ Living room includes a fireplace and built-in bookshelves.

✔ Generous closet space is incorporated into the master bath/dressing area.

Plan number LWG-1088-SU93. See index for price details. Plan by Larry W. Garnett & Associates Inc.

The diagrams presented here constitute only floor plans and elevations. Purchasers are advised to consult their state and local building regulations and a state-certified architect prior to any construction related to these plans.

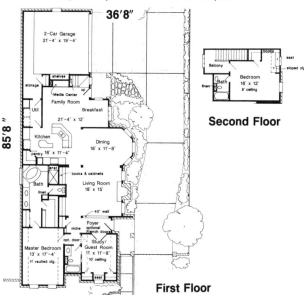

36'8"

2-Car Garage
21'-4" x 19'-4"

shelves

storage

Media Center
Family Room
21'-4" x 12'

Breakfast

Util

Kitchen

pantry

Dining
16' x 11'-8"

Bath

linen

books & cabinets

Living Room
18' x 15'

niche

40" wall

Foyer
optional french doors

Bath

opt. door

Master Bedroom
13' x 17'-4"
1f vaulted clg.

Study/
Guest Room
11' x 11'-8"
10' ceiling

seat

85'8"

First Floor

doors

seat

sloped clg.

Balcony

Bath

Bedroom
16' x 12'
8' ceiling

linen

Second Floor

Versatile Loft
Can Be Finished
As An Extra Bedroom

First floor—896 sq. ft.
Second floor—892 sq. ft.
Total living space—1788 sq. ft.
3-4 bedrooms, 2½ baths
Shown with a concrete slab

- The plan's narrow footprint makes it suitable for narrow-lot or high-density applications.

- Sliding-glass doors give both the living and family rooms access to the patio.

- A breakfast nook is included in the kitchen.

Plan number QJA-1911-8907. See index for pricing details. Plan by Quincy Johnson & Associates.

The diagrams presented here constitute only floor plans and elevations. Purchasers are advised to consult their state and local building regulations and a state-certified architect prior to any construction related to these plans.

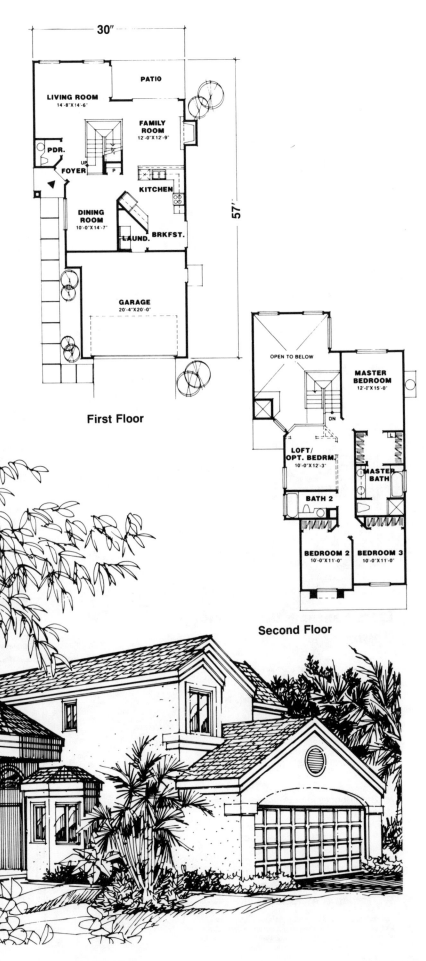

First Floor

Second Floor

Code: DIFF   To Order, Phone Toll Free 1-800-323-7379

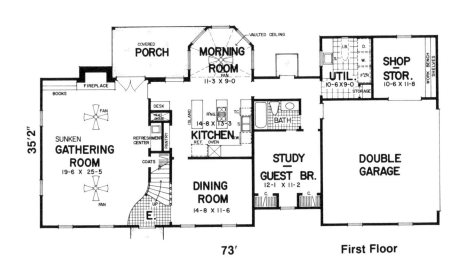

73' **First Floor**

35'2"

Second Floor

Simple Exterior Lines
Belie Exciting Plan Within

First floor—1677 sq. ft.
Second floor—1025 sq. ft.
Total living space—2702 sq. ft.
3-4 bedrooms, 3 baths
Shown with a concrete slab or
crawlspace

✔ Plan cannot be sold or built in the state
of Tennessee.

✔ Sunken gathering room, directly off the
entry, features a fireplace, recessed wet
bar, a built-in bookcase and French
doors leading to a screened porch.

✔ The central location of the kitchen,
between the dining area and morning
room, makes it easy to serve guests in
either room.

✔ The kitchen boasts a cooking island and
a snack bar island.

**Plan number RJA-M2202-8905. See
index for pricing details. Plan by
Ralph Jones & Associates.**

The diagrams presented here constitute only floor plans
and elevations. Purchasers are advised to consult their
state and local building regulations and a state-certified
architect prior to any construction related to these plans.

Exterior Elements, Oversized Windows Create West Coast Wonder

First floor—1350 sq. ft.
Second floor—1108 sq. ft.
Total living space—2458 sq. ft.
4 bedrooms, 2½ baths
Shown with a crawlspace or concrete slab

- ✔ Covered porch opens to spacious foyer with elegant staircase.

- ✔ Two-way fireplace is shared by formal and informal living areas.

- ✔ French doors lead from the master bedroom to a private deck. A second private deck is off the master bath.

- ✔ Skylights brighten both second-floor baths.

Plan number DPI-M2302-8906. See index for pricing details. Plan by Design Profile Inc.

The diagrams presented here constitute only floor plans and elevations. Purchasers are advised to consult their state and local building regulations and a state-certified architect prior to any construction related to these plans.

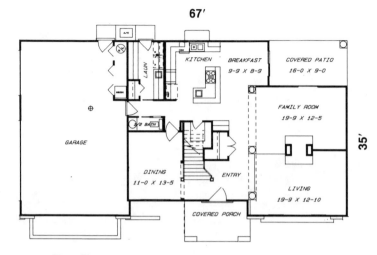

67'

35'

GARAGE

1/2 BATH

LAUN

KITCHEN

BREAKFAST
9-9 X 8-9

COVERED PATIO
16-0 X 9-0

FAMILY ROOM
19-9 X 12-5

DINING
11-0 X 13-5

ENTRY

LIVING
19-9 X 12-10

COVERED PORCH

First Floor

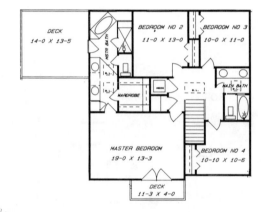

DECK
14-0 X 13-5

MSTR BATH

BEDROOM NO 2
11-0 X 13-0

BEDROOM NO 3
10-0 X 11-0

WARDROBE

MAIN BATH

MASTER BEDROOM
19-0 X 13-3

BEDROOM NO 4
10-10 X 10-6

DECK
11-3 X 4-0

Second Floor

Dramatic Foyer Says Welcome Into Spacious Living Room

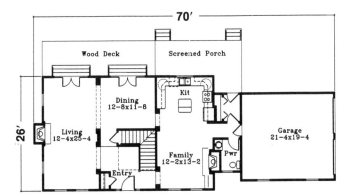

First Floor

Second Floor

First floor—1164 sq. ft.
Second floor—956 sq. ft.
Total living space—2120 sq. ft.
3-4 bedrooms, 2½ baths
Shown with a basement

- ✔ Spacious kitchen/family room is comfortable and inviting.

- ✔ Outdoor entertaining is encouraged by a rear wood deck and screened porch.

- ✔ Family room fireplace includes built-in bookshelves and log storage.

- ✔ Library is surrounded by bookshelves and includes an engaging window seat.

- ✔ Master suite has a private bath, walk-in closet.

Plan number EDI-1490-SU93. See index for price details. Plan by EDI Architecture/Planning.

The diagrams presented here constitute only floor plans and elevations. Purchasers are advised to consult their state and local building regulations and a state-certified architect prior to any construction related to these plans.

New England Colonial
Ideal For Rest of Country

First floor—1000 sq. ft.
Second floor—968 sq. ft.
Total living space—1968 sq. ft.
4 bedrooms, 2½ baths
Shown with a basement

✔ Stately New England Colonial has a columned porch, clapboard sliding and elliptical window.

✔ Island kitchen and breakfast area open to family room and rear deck, bay window and skylight brighten family room, while drama is added with cathedral ceiling.

✔ Second-floor master suite includes a his-and-her walk-in closet, whirlpool tub and separate shower stall, and a double vanity.

✔ Mud/laundry room separate garage from foyer. Foyer also includes a convenient powder room.

✔ An attached deck off the kitchen provides easy access to outdoor dining in favorable weather. A formal dining room is also adjacent to kitchen.

Plan number ORC-2997-AJ92. See index for pricing details. Plan by Orchard House.

The diagrams presented here constitute only floor plans and elevations. Purchasers are advised to consult their state and local building regulations and a state-certified architect prior to any construction related to these plans.

Second Floor

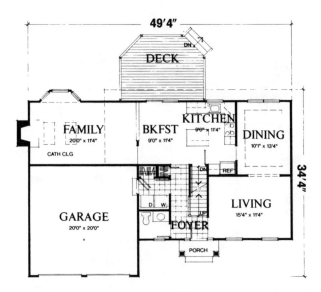

First Floor

First-Floor Master Wing Is Very Private

First floor—1815 sq. ft.
Second floor—897 sq. ft.
Total living space—2712 sq. ft.
4 bedrooms, 2½ baths
Shown with a basement

✔ The garage wing balances the private first-floor master suite on this classic Georgian house.

✔ The center entry classically balances the formal dining room on one side and the formal living room on the other.

✔ The island kitchen shares space with the breakfast area which includes a pantry and planning desk. A half wall separates the kitchen/breakfast from the double-high family room.

✔ Upstairs an open loft area overlooks the family room. There are three bedrooms and a full bathroom on that level.

✔ The first-floor master suite is large enough for a private sitting area. The master bathroom features a large bathtub, a separate shower, large walk-in closet and a dual vanity with dressing table.

Plan number ORC-2991-AJ92. See index for pricing details. Plan by Orchard House.

The diagrams presented here constitute only floor plans and elevations. Purchasers are advised to consult their state and local building regulations and a state-certified architect prior to any construction related to these plans.

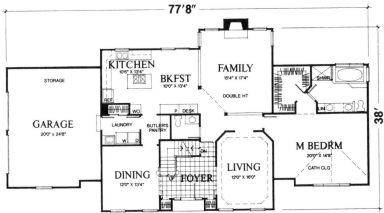

First Floor

Second Floor

Elevation B: TDC-122B-92DC

Elevation C: TDC-122C-92DC

Elevation A: TDC-122A-92DC

Elevation D: TDC-122D-92DC

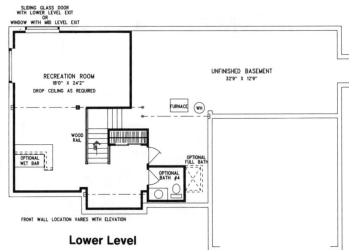

SLIDING GLASS DOOR
WITH LOWER LEVEL EXIT
OR
WINDOW WITH MID LEVEL EXIT

RECREATION ROOM
18'0" X 24'2"

DROP CEILING AS REQUIRED

UNFINISHED BASEMENT
32'9" X 12'9"

FURNACE   WH

WOOD
RAIL

OPTIONAL
WET BAR

OPTIONAL
BATH #4

OPTIONAL
FULL BATH

FRONT WALL LOCATION VARIES WITH ELEVATION

Lower Level

Second Level with 8' high 1st floor ceilings

54'

34'

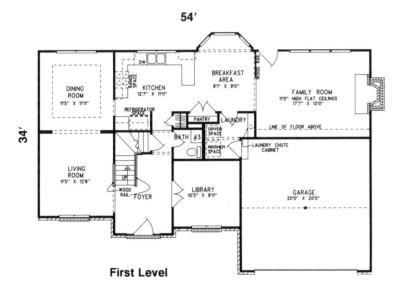

First Level

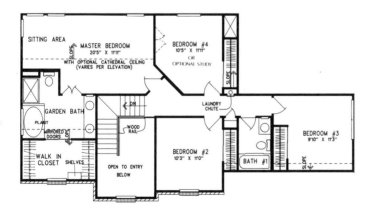

Second Level with optional 9' 1st floor high ceilings

The Bennington

Elevation A:
First floor—1196 sq. ft.
Second floor—1045 sq. ft.
Total living space—2241 sq. ft.

Elevation B:
First floor—1183 sq. ft.
Second floor—1045 sq. ft.
Total living space—2228 sq. ft.

Elevation C:
First floor—1183 sq. ft.
Second floor—1045 sq. ft.
Total living space—2228 sq. ft.

Elevation D:
First floor—1188 sq. ft.
Second floor—1052 sq. ft.
Total living space—2240 sq. ft.

All elevations:
4 bedrooms, 2½ baths
Plan includes a basement

✔ Plan order includes both second floor choices.

✔ Guests are greeted by a two-story entry.

✔ The family room is separated from the breakfast area by a wood railing. The room features an eleven-foot ceiling, a fireplace, and access to outside.

✔ Adjacent to the kitchen is the breakfast area which includes a bay window.

✔ Enter the master bedroom through double doors and enjoy the many luxuries. The room features a sitting area and a private bath that includes a garden tub.

✔ The first floor laundry features a laundry chute.

Please order each elevation separately. See index for price details. Plan by The Drees Company.

The diagrams presented here constitute only floor plans and elevations. Purchasers are advised to consult their state and local building regulations and a state-certified architect prior to any construction related to these plans.

Formal, Informal Living Areas Dress Traditional Two Story Up Or Down

First floor—1122 sq. ft.
Second floor—962 sq. ft.
Total living space—2084 sq. ft.
3 bedrooms, 2½ baths
Shown with a concrete slab

- The living and dining rooms flank the central foyer.

- The large family room includes a fireplace and access to the backyard reception area.

- The master bath is especially comfortable with its separate shower and spa tub.

- The hall bath, which serves the secondary bedrooms, features an efficient, compartmented layout.

Plan number EDI-1489-89MM. See index for pricing details. Plan by EDI Architecture/Planning.

The diagrams presented here constitute only floor plans and elevations. Purchasers are advised to consult their state and local building regulations and a state-certified architect prior to any construction related to these plans.

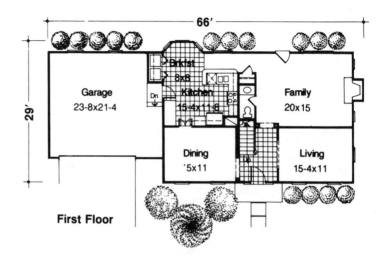

First Floor

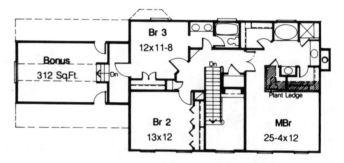

Second Floor

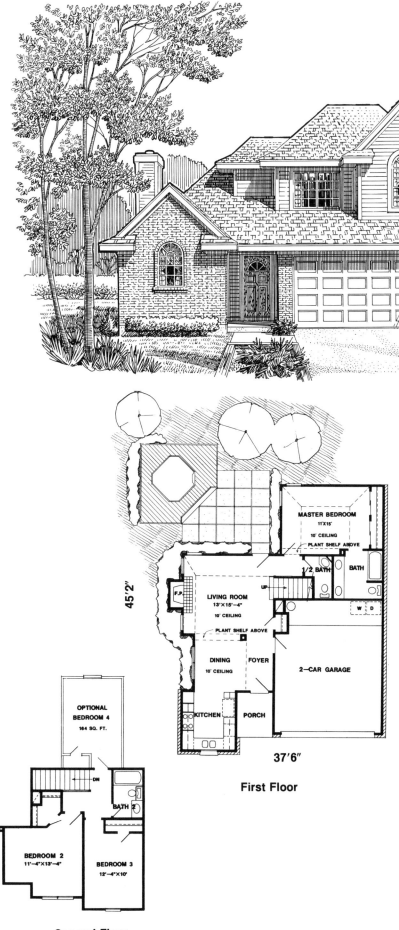

MASTER BEDROOM
11'X15'
10' CEILING
PLANT SHELF ABOVE

1/2 BATH

BATH

F.P.

LIVING ROOM
13'X15'-4"
10' CEILING

UP

W   D

PLANT SHELF ABOVE

DINING
10' CEILING

FOYER

2-CAR GARAGE

KITCHEN

PORCH

45'2"

37'6"

First Floor

OPTIONAL BEDROOM 4
164 SQ. FT.

DN

BATH 2

BEDROOM 2
11'-4"X13'-4"

BEDROOM 3
12'-4"X10'

Second Floor

First-Floor Master Suite Suits Move-Down Buyers

First floor—838 sq. ft.
Second floor—453 sq. ft.
Total living space—1291 sq. ft.
3 bedrooms, 2½ baths
Shown with a concrete slab

✔ The covered porch opens to a formal foyer.

✔ The kitchen is open to the dining room.

✔ Columns and a plant shelf separate the living room from the dining room.

✔ The living room has a fireplace and access to a rear patio.

✔ The master suite has a vaulted ceiling, plant shelf and private bath.

Plan number LWG-1002-91ZZ. See index for pricing details. Plan by Larry Garnett & Associates Inc.

The diagrams presented here constitute only floor plans and elevations. Purchasers are advised to consult their state and local building regulations and a state-certified architect prior to any construction related to these plans.

Variety of Built-Ins Entertaining Spaces Highlight Design

**Total living space—1935 sq. ft.
3 bedrooms, baths
Shown with a concrete slab**

✔ Home has a variety of private outdoor living spaces, including a dining terrace, a patio, and a side porch with fountain.

✔ Large living room includes a built-in media center, fireplace, and atrium doors that lead to the patio.

✔ Skylights brighten the master bath and library. Other extras include built-in bookshelves in the foyer and library, and a corner hutch in the dining room.

✔ In addition to large bedroom closets, other storage potential exists in the large two-car garage, a utility closet, and the linen closet in the master bath.

Plan number LWG-1008-91ZZ. See index for pricing details. Plan by Larry W. Garnett & Associates Inc.

The diagrams presented here constitute only floor plans and elevations. Purchasers are advised to consult their state and local building regulations and a state-certified architect prior to any construction related to these plans.

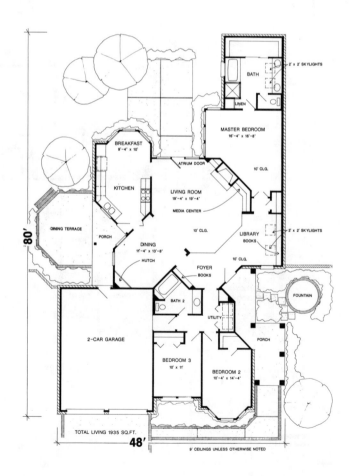

Main Floor

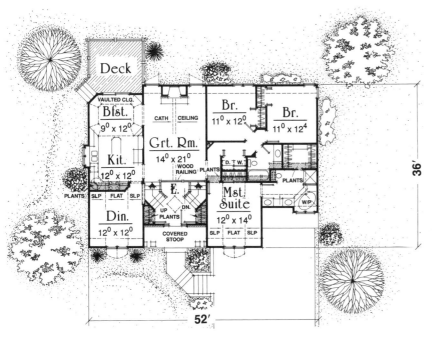

Separate Spaces
Double Dining Pleasure
In Three-Bedroom Ranch

Total living space—1646 sq. ft.
3 bedrooms, 2 baths
Shown with a basement

✔ Eye-catching gazebo ceiling defines the breakfast area incorporated into the elongated kitchen.

✔ Two closets provide much appreciated storage space in the foyer.

✔ Master bath offers an exciting corner location for a whirlpool tub, plus a separate shower.

✔ Soaring cathedral ceiling increases visual space in the central great room.

Plan number CCI-2606-91M5. See index for pricing details. Plan by Custom Creations Inc.

The diagrams presented here constitute only floor plans and elevations. Purchasers are advised to consult their state and local building regulations and a state-certified architect prior to any construction related to these plans.

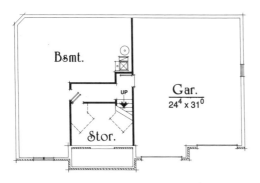

Skylights Make
Dining Room Shine

First floor—737 sq. ft.
Second floor—685 sq. ft.
Total living space—1422 sq. ft.
3 bedrooms, 2½ baths
Shown with a basement

- The parlor, warmed by a fireplace, creates a cozy retreat to unwind.

- The family room features access to the deck.

- The U-shaped kitchen opens to the dining room that is brightened with skylights and looks out to the deck.

- The master bedroom, located on the second floor, features a compartmented bath and his-and-her closets.

- The second floor laundry room is an added convenience to household chores.

Plan number TGC-503-9104. See index for pricing details. Plan by The Garlinghouse Co.

The diagrams presented here constitute only floor plans and elevations. Purchasers are advised to consult their state and local building regulations and a state-certified architect prior to any construction related to these plans.

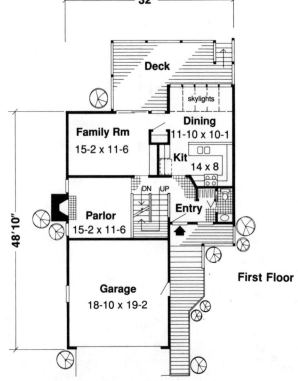

First Floor

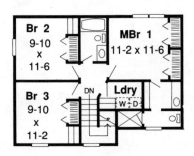

Second Floor

Rear Elevation

34'4"

74'10"

MASTER BEDROOM
16'-0"x13'-0"

COVERED PATIO

MASTER BATH

LIVING ROOM
20'-0"x14'-3"

UP

FOYER

DINING ROOM
12'-0"x11'-7"

BREAKFAST

KITCHEN

GARAGE
20'-0"x18'-0"

First Floor

34'-4"

56'-2"

MASTER BEDROOM BELOW

LOFT
16'-9"x 14'-0"

OPEN

DN

OPEN

BEDROOM 3
12'-6"x11'-6"

BEDROOM 2
12'-6"x10'-0"

BATH 1

Second Floor

Design Is Ideal For Small, One-Sided Lots

First floor—1243 sq. ft.
Second floor—710 sq. ft.
Total living space—1953 sq. ft.
3 bedrooms, 2½ baths
Shown with a concrete slab

↳ Two-story plan is designed for first-floor living for owners or parents, with guests or children upstairs.

↳ Master bedroom suite includes a large walk-in closet; master bedroom features a double-sink vanity, a compartmented toilet, and a corner tub.

↳ Upstairs loft is open to living room below.

↳ Home has a covered porch in front; in the rear, a spacious living room opens to a covered patio.

Plan number QJA-1986-AJ92. See index for pricing details. Plan by Quincy Johnson & Associates.

The diagrams presented here constitute only floor plans and elevations. Purchasers are advised to consult their state and local building regulations and a state-certified architect prior to any construction related to these plans.

Three Bedroom A Good Match For Corner Lot

First floor—560 sq. ft.
Second floor—790 sq. ft.
Total living space—1350 sq. ft.
3 bedrooms, 2½ baths
Shown with a crawlspace

- ✔ Shallow depth of the plan makes it suitable for smaller lots.

- ✔ Master suite has a private bath. Bedroom two may serve as a second master suite.

- ✔ Each bedroom has a walk-in closet.

- ✔ Living room features a fireplace as a focus.

- ✔ Snack bar separates the kitchen and dining area.

Plan number AMA-2498-SU93. See index for price details. Plan by Alan Mascord Design Associates.

The diagrams presented here constitute only floor plans and elevations. Purchasers are advised to consult their state and local building regulations and a state-certified architect prior to any construction related to these plans.

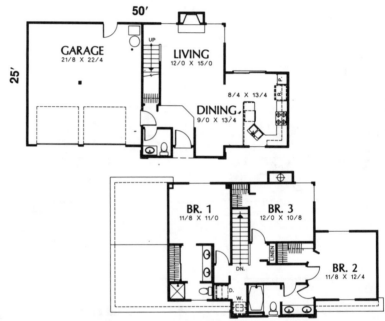

All-Brick Neo-Traditional Home Fits Very Narrow Lot

Total living space—889 sq. ft.
2 bedrooms, 2 baths
Shown with a crawlspace

- ✔ The covered porch, arched-topped and clerestory windows add charm to this smaller home.

- ✔ Inside, the great room has a sloped ceiling and room for a dining area.

- ✔ A patio, off of the great room, adds outdoor living space.

Decorative Brickwork Has Elegant Street Appeal

First Floor

73'

51'

Second Floor

First floor—1820 sq. ft.
Second floor—1384 sq. ft.
Total living space—3204 sq. ft.
3 bedrooms, 2½ baths
Shown with a crawlspace

✔ Island kitchen has a built-in phone desk, a walk-in pantry and overlooks the breakfast nook and family room.

✔ Master suite includes a private study complete with fireplace and decorative ceiling treatments.

✔ The formal living and dining rooms have tray ceilings. The living room has a fireplace and access to the front walkway.

✔ The family room has a fireplace and access to the backyard.

✔ The master bath has his-and-her vanities, a compartmented toilet and a large walk-in closet/dressing area.

Plan number AMA-L2414-9110. See index for pricing details. Plan by Alan Mascord Design Associates.

The diagrams presented here constitute only floor plans and elevations. Purchasers are advised to consult their state and local building regulations and a state-certified architect prior to any construction related to these plans.

✔ The efficient kitchen includes an eating bar, pantry and room for a washer and dryer.

✔ The master suite has a large closet and a private bath.

Plan number RJA-2201-91ZZ. See index for pricing details. Plan by Ralph Jones & Associates.

The diagrams presented here constitute only floor plans and elevations. Purchasers are advised to consult their state and local building regulations and a state-certified architect prior to any construction related to these plans.

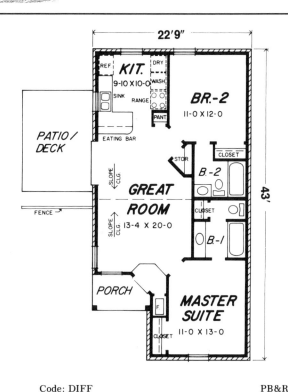

Neo-Traditional Home Fits Snugly On A Narrow Lot

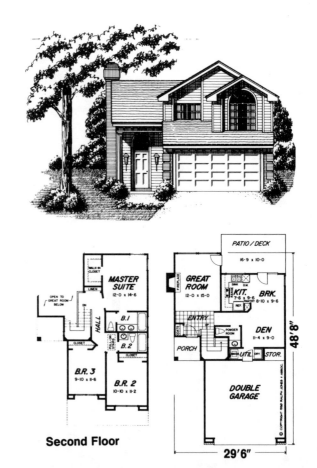

First floor—675 sq. ft.
Second floor—723 sq. ft.
Total living space—1398 sq. ft.
3 bedrooms, 2½ baths
Shown on concrete slab

✔ The fully equipped kitchen provides room for food preparation and adjoins the breakfast area.

✔ The great room has a fireplace and abundant space for family gatherings.

✔ The master bedroom has a walk-in closet. The bath contains a compartmented toilet and a double-bowled vanity.

Plan number RJA-2207-9108. See index for pricing details. Plan by Ralph Jones & Associates.

The diagrams presented here constitute only floor plans and elevations. Purchasers are advised to consult their state and local building regulations and a state-certified architect prior to any construction related to these plans.

Second Floor

First Floor

First-Time Buyers Find Added Amenities

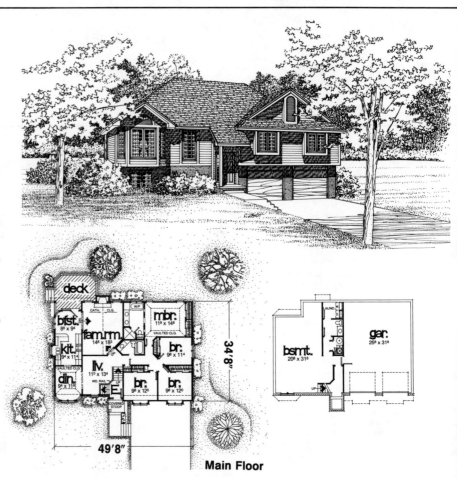

Total living space—1665 sq. ft.
4 bedrooms, 2½ baths
Shown with a basement

✔ Master suite has a vaulted ceiling and plenty of closet space. The bath has dual vanities, a whirlpool tub and a separate shower.

✔ The sunken family room has a cathedral ceiling and a fireplace.

✔ The kitchen has plenty of counter space and a snack bar. The sunlit breakfast room has access to the rear deck.

✔ The formal dining room has a vaulted ceiling. The living room has a decorative wood railing.

Plan number CCI-2628-9207. See index for pricing details. Plan by Custom Creations Inc.

The diagrams presented here constitute only floor plans and elevations. Purchasers are advised to consult their state and local building regulations and a state-certified architect prior to any construction related to these plans.

Main Floor

First Floor

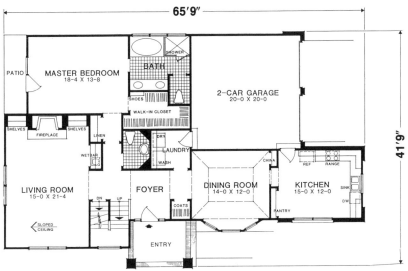

65'9"

41'9"

PATIO

MASTER BEDROOM
18-4 X 13-8

BATH

SHOWER

2-CAR GARAGE
20-0 X 20-0

SHOES

WALK-IN CLOSET

SHELVES   FIREPLACE   SHELVES

LINEN

DRY
WASH

LAUNDRY

CHINA

REF   RANGE

WETBAR

LIVING ROOM
15-0 X 21-4

FOYER

DINING ROOM
14-0 X 12-0

KITCHEN
15-0 X 12-0

SINK

DW

DN   UP

SLOPED
CEILING

COATS

PANTRY

ENTRY

First Floor

Second Floor

BEDROOM #3
14-8 X 13-8

TRAY CEILING

TOWELS

BEDROOM #2
16-0 X 15-0

TRAY CEILING

SHELVES

W.I. CLOSET

W.I. CLOSET

LINEN   LAUN.
CHUTE

BALCONY

ATTIC STORAGE

OPEN TO LIVING ROOM BELOW

DN

SOLID RAIL

OPEN TO
FOYER
BELOW

Second Floor

Smooth Flowing Plan Makes Entertaining Or Relaxing A Pleasure

First floor—1574 sq. ft.
Second floor—906 sq. ft.
Total living space—2480 sq. ft.
3 bedrooms, 3½ baths
Plan includes a basement

- ✔ Central foyer opens to either the living room or the dining room.

- ✔ Large living area includes a sloped ceiling and a fireplace flanked by bookshelves.

- ✔ A coffered ceiling, china hutch and a bay window accent the dining room.

- ✔ Master bedroom has access to a private patio.

Plan number TNG-M391-89MM. See index for pricing details. Plan by The Norris Group Inc.

The diagrams presented here constitute only floor plans and elevations. Purchasers are advised to consult their state and local building regulations and a state-certified architect prior to any construction related to these plans.

Rear Elevation

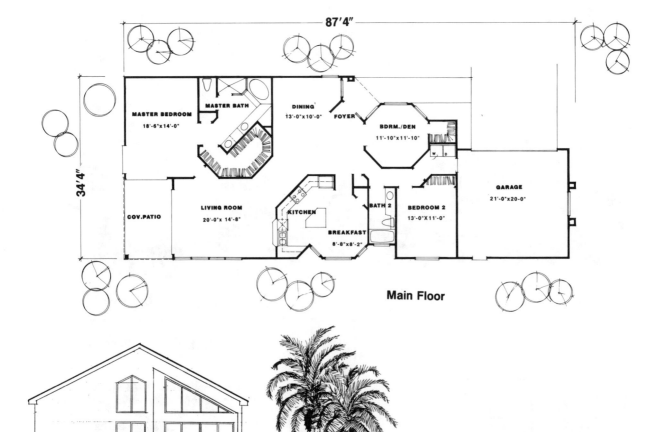

87'4"

34'4"

MASTER BEDROOM
18'-6"x14'-0"

MASTER BATH

DINING
13'-0"x10'-0"

FOYER

BDRM./DEN
11'-10"x11'-10"

COV.PATIO

LIVING ROOM
20'-0" x 14'-8"

KITCHEN

BATH 2

BEDROOM 2
13'-0"X11'-0"

BREAKFAST
8'-8"x8'-2"

GARAGE
21'-0"x20-0"

Main Floor

Rear Elevation

Mission-Style Golf Course House On Zero-Lot Line

**Total living space—1870 sq. ft.
3 bedrooms, 2 baths
Shown with a concrete slab**

✔ ''Zero-lot line'' patio home is an ideal golf lifestyle home for the empty nester. Included in this three bedroom home is an octagon-shaped den/bedroom.

✔ Flowing plan comes with a dining room and living room. Bay windows and vaulted ceilings offer design intrigue.

✔ Master suite comes with very large walk-in closet, separate tub and shower, and enclosed toilet.

Order each elevation separately. See index for pricing details. Plan by Quincy Johnson & Associates.

The diagrams presented here constitute only floor plans and elevations. Purchasers are advised to consult their state and local building regulations and a state-certified architect prior to any construction related to these plans.

Plan number QJA-1998-AJ92

Plan number QJA-1997-AJ92

34'2"

73'

MASTER BATH

MASTER BEDROOM
14-0 X 17-4

WALK-IN CLOSET

WET BAR

PDR. ROOM

LIVING ROOM
12-8 X 15-0

ATRIUM

DINING ROOM
8-10 X 11-4

BREAKFAST
7-2 X 8-0

BEDROOM 2
12-0 X 10-8

REF

P

KITCHEN

FOYER

LAUNDRY
ROOM

ENTRY

PLANTER

GARAGE
20-0 X 20-0

Main Floor

All-Glass Atrium Provides Attractive Interior Green Space

**Total living space—1973 sq. ft.
2 bedrooms, 2½ baths
Shown with a concrete slab**

✔ Convenient coat closet is included in the foyer.

✔ Breakfast area, dining room and powder room all have a view of the atrium.

✔ Living and dining rooms share space, and a view of the corner fireplace.

✔ Skylit, dual-basin vanity is included in the very comfortable master bath.

✔ Bedroom two features a private, full bath.

Plan number QJA-M1901-8805. See index for pricing details. Plan by Quincy Johnson & Associates.

The diagrams presented here constitute only floor plans and elevations. Purchasers are advised to consult their state and local building regulations and a state-certified architect prior to any construction related to these plans.

Generous Closet Space Gives All Three Bedrooms Extra Appeal

First floor—1019 sq. ft.
Second floor—800 sq. ft.
Total living space—1819 sq. ft.
Unfinished basement—684 sq. ft.
3 bedrooms, 2½ baths
Shown with a basement

- ✔ Vaulted ceilings are featured in the foyer, kitchen and living and dining rooms. They are optional for the second floor.

- ✔ Sunken family room is open to the kitchen/breakfast area.

- ✔ Extra cabinets are included in the walk-through laundry room.

- ✔ Sliding door closes the formal dining area off from the kitchen.

- ✔ Practical central powder room serves the main floor.

Plan number DPI-2399-SU93. See index for price details. Plan by Design Profile Inc.

The diagrams presented here constitute only floor plans and elevations. Purchasers are advised to consult their state and local building regulations and a state-certified architect prior to any construction related to these plans.

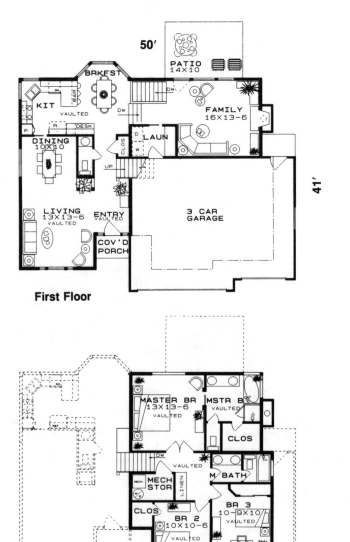

First Floor

Second Floor

Copyright 1992 Stephen S. Fuller, Inc.

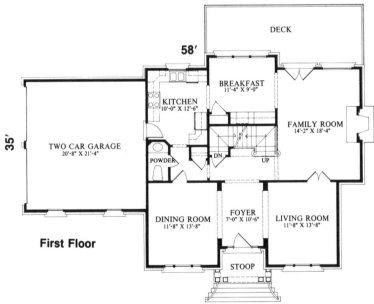

First Floor

DECK

58'

35'

BREAKFAST
11'-4" X 9'-0"

KITCHEN
10'-0" X 12'-6"

FAMILY ROOM
14'-2" X 18'-4"

TWO CAR GARAGE
20'-8" X 21'-4"

POWDER

DN.   UP

DINING ROOM
11'-8" X 13'-8"

FOYER
7'-0" X 10'-6"

LIVING ROOM
11'-8" X 13'-8"

STOOP

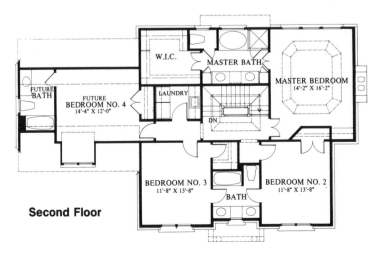

Second Floor

W.I.C.

MASTER BATH

MASTER BEDROOM
14'-2" X 16'-2"

FUTURE
BATH

FUTURE
BEDROOM NO. 4
14'-4" X 12'-0"

LAUNDRY

DN.

BEDROOM NO. 3
11'-8" X 13'-8"

BATH

BEDROOM NO. 2
11'-8" X 13'-8"

Family, Friends Will All Feel At Home In Three-Bedroom Two Story

First floor—1165 sq. ft.
Second floor—1050 sq. ft.
Total living space—2215 sq. ft.
3-4 bedrooms, 2½-3½ baths
Shown with a basement

✔ Living and dining rooms provide the space for entertaining.

✔ French doors in the family room open onto a deck.

✔ Large breakfast room, with a pantry, adjoins the kitchen.

✔ Generous closet space is provided in the bedrooms.

✔ Expansion space for an additional bedroom is available over the garage.

Plan number DTA-2599-SU93. See index for price details. Plan by Design Traditions.

The diagrams presented here constitute only floor plans and elevations. Purchasers are advised to consult their state and local building regulations and a state-certified architect prior to any construction related to these plans.

Luxury Details Abound In Elegant Georgian

First floor—2360 sq. ft.
Second floor—1097 sq. ft.
Total living space—3457 sq. ft.
3 bedrooms, 3½ baths
Shown with a concrete slab or crawl space

- ✔ Plan cannot be sold or built in the state of Tennessee.

- ✔ The dining room and living room each feature a decorative mansard ceiling and their own fireplaces. The home has a third fireplace in the family room.

- ✔ The master suite features separate his-and-her closets in the bath, stained glass over the tub, and a linen closet.

- ✔ Upstairs, the second bedroom is brightened by skylights, has its own walk-in closet, and a window seat in the dormer (as does the third bedroom).

- ✔ A large utility area has a space for a wash-up sink, washer/dryer and a freezer. The home's many storage possibilities include a large pantry and extra closet space under the back stairs.

Plan number RJA-2207-91ZZ. See index for pricing details. Plan by Ralph Jones & Associates.

The diagrams presented here constitute only floor plans and elevations. Purchasers are advised to consult their state and local building regulations and a state-certified architect prior to any construction related to these plans.

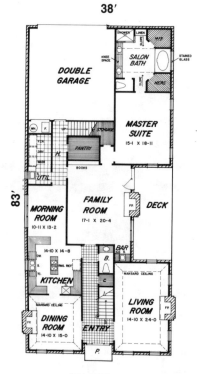

First Floor   **Second Floor**

BASEMENT PLAN

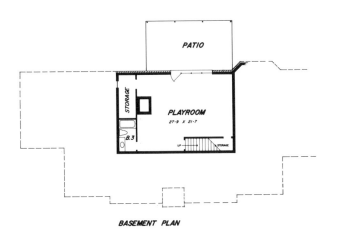

Sprawling Traditional Encompasses Contemporary Amenities

Total living space—2595 sq. ft.
Basement—804 sq. ft.
(not included in total)
3 bedrooms, 2½ baths
Shown with a basement or crawl space

✔ Plan cannot be sold or built in the state of Tennessee

✔ Master salon bath includes a step-up bathtub, corner shower, and his-and-her walk-in closets.

✔ The master bedroom, second and third bedrooms feature walk-in closets as well.

✔ Island kitchen has an eating bar, hutch and menu planning desk. It offers convenient access to formal dining room as well as sunny morning room.

✔ Spacious great room has fireplace, built-in bookshelves and an oversized ceiling fan.

Plan number RJA-M2231-90MN. See index for pricing details. Plan by Ralph Jones & Associates.

The diagrams presented here constitute only floor plans and elevations. Purchasers are advised to consult their state and local building regulations and a state-certified architect prior to any construction related to these plans.

Compact Narrow-Lot Design

First floor—675 sq. ft.
Second floor—723 sq. ft.
Total living space—1398 sq. ft.
3 bedrooms, 3 baths
Shown with a concrete slab or crawlspace

- ✔ Plan cannot be sold or built in the state of Tennessee.

- ✔ The master bedroom features a walk-in closet, while the master bathroom has dual-basin sinks, a compartmented toilet and a separate tub.

- ✔ The home's second and third bedrooms are upstairs, and share a second bathroom.

- ✔ The rear patio/deck can be accessed both from the breakfast room as well as the great room.

- ✔ The U-shaped kitchen has a pantry, offers window views from the sink, and is in close proximity to the den.

Plan number RJA-2205-91ZZ. See index for pricing details. Plan by Ralph Jones & Associates.

The diagrams presented here constitute only floor plans and elevations. Purchasers are advised to consult their state and local building regulations and a state-certified architect prior to any construction related to these plans.

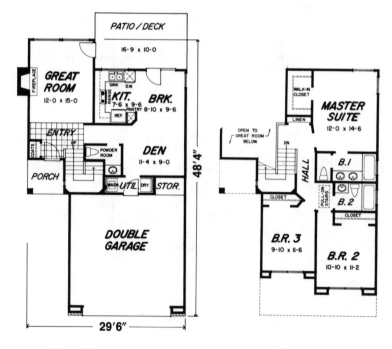

First Floor

Second Floor

Floor Plans

Second Floor

SALON BATH

MASTER SUITE
24'-0" X 18'-2"
MANSARD CEILING

BEDROOM #4
20'-7" X 13'-0"

B2

HALL

BALCONY

BEDROOM #2
14'-0" X 18'-0"

GRAND HALL BELOW

PLANT SHELF

BEDROOM #3
16'-0" X 20'-0"
MANSARD CEILING

B3

ATTIC ACCESS

Second Floor

First Floor

DOUBLE GARAGE

44'

84'

GUEST BR.
13'-0" X 12'-0"

H.

B.4

MORNING ROOM
14'-0" X 13'-8"

PATIO/DECK

GAME ROOM
14'-0" X 21'-0"

KIT.
14'-0" X 13'-0"

EATING BAR

FAMILY ROOM
16'-0" X 21'-0"

DINING ROOM
14'-0" X 18'-0"

GRAND HALL

B.

LIBRARY
16'-0" X 12'-0"

BOOKS

First Floor

Exciting Plan Mixes Recreation With Opulence

First floor—2272 sq. ft.
Second floor—2496 sq. ft.
Total living space—4768 sq. ft.
5 bedrooms, 4½ baths
Shown with a concrete slab or crawlspace

- Plan cannot be built or sold in the state of Tennessee.

- The elegant two-story grand hall is highlighted by a curving stairway.

- The first-floor game room has its own fireplace, a storage closet, and a refreshment center supplied from the kitchen.

- The spectacular skylit master bath has separate makeup areas, linen shelves and walk-in closets, a step-up tub, a compartmented toilet, plant shelves and stained glass windows.

- Most of the bedrooms have their own walk-in closets. Other storage possibilities include two pantries in the kitchen, built-in bookshelves in the family room and the master bedroom, and a large utility room near the double garage.

Plan number RJA-2203-91ZZ. See index for pricing details. Plan by Ralph Jones & Associates.

The diagrams presented here constitute only floor plans and elevations. Purchasers are advised to consult their state and local building regulations and a state-certified architect prior to any construction related to these plans.

Bay Windows Add Appeal Inside And Out

First floor—1080 sq. ft.
Second floor—960 sq. ft.
Total living space—2040 sq. ft.
4 bedrooms, 2½ baths
Shown with a basement

- Kitchen, breakfast area and family room share visual space.

- Bay windows highlight the living and formal dining rooms.

- Master bath includes a separate tub and shower and a linen closet.

- Secondary bedrooms are comfortable, share a functional hall bath.

- Large laundry room doubles as a mud room.

Plan number TCB-1293-SU93. See index for price details. Plan by Barton & Associates, Inc.

The diagrams presented here constitute only floor plans and elevations. Purchasers are advised to consult their state and local building regulations and a state-certified architect prior to any construction related to these plans.

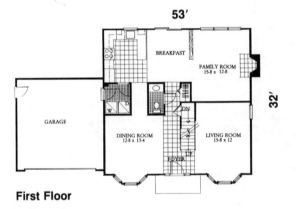

First Floor

Informal Family Area Will Be Most Used In The Home

First floor—1333 sq. ft.
Second floor—1567 sq. ft.
Total living space—2900 sq. ft.
5 bedrooms, 2½ baths
Shown with a basement

- Open arrangement of the kitchen, family room and breakfast area creates a large, comfortable informal zone.

- Fireplace serves as a focal point in the family room.

- Private sitting area is included in the master suite.

- Each of the four secondary bedrooms offers plenty of space.

- Spacious laundry room includes a handy sink.

Plan number TCB-1299-SU93. See index for price details. Plan by Barton & Associates, Inc.

The diagrams presented here constitute only floor plans and elevations. Purchasers are advised to consult their state and local building regulations and a state-certified architect prior to any construction related to these plans.

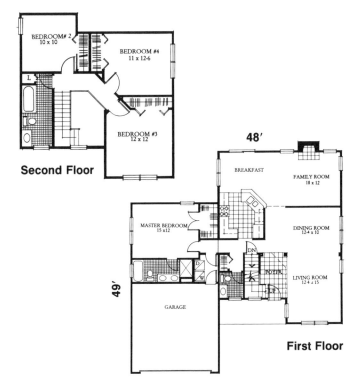

Second Floor

BEDROOM# 2
10 x 10

BEDROOM #4
11 x 12-6

BEDROOM #3
12 x 12

48'

BREAKFAST

FAMILY ROOM
18 x 12

MASTER BEDROOM
15 x12

DINING ROOM
12-4 x 10

49'

FOYER

LIVING ROOM
12-4 x 15

GARAGE

First Floor

Soaring Foyer Ceiling Serves As A Dramatic Opening Statement

First floor—1358 sq. ft.
Second floor—601 sq. ft.
Total living space—1959 sq. ft.
4 bedrooms, 2½ baths
Shown with a basement

- Two-story ceiling in the foyer opens up the home's interior living spaces.

- Kitchen, breakfast nook and family room share visual space.

- Master bath includes a separate tub and shower.

- Secondary bedrooms occupy the second floor.

- Second-floor hall is open fully to enhance the foyer's ceiling treatment

Plan number TCB-1291-SU93. See index for price details. Plan by Barton & Associates, Inc.

The diagrams presented here constitute only floor plans and elevations. Purchasers are advised to consult their state and local building regulations and a state-certified architect prior to any construction related to these plans.

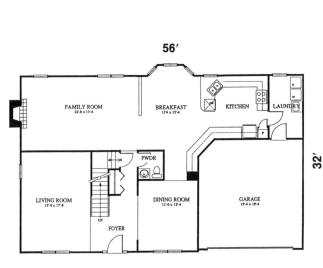

BATH
OPT LAV

MASTER BATH

LIN

BEDROOM #2
17-0 x 17-0

BEDROOM #3
14'-0 x 17-4

Walk In Closet

LIN

DN

Plant Shelf

OPEN

MASTER BEDROOM
17-0 x 14-4

BEDROOM #4
17-0 x 14-4

BEDROOM # 5
19'-4 x 17-0

SITTING AREA
9'-4 x 9-8

Second Floor

56'

FAMILY ROOM
22-8 x 17-4

BREAKFAST
11'4 x 17-4

KITCHEN

LAUNDRY

32'

DN

PWDR

LIVING ROOM
17-0 x 17-8

DINING ROOM
11'-0 x 17-4

GARAGE
19'-4 x 19'-4

UP

FOYER

First Floor

Elevation A: TDC-106A-92DC

Elevation C: TDC-106C-92DC

The Baycroft

Elevation A:
Total living space—1126 sq. ft.
Elevation B:
Total living space—1106 sq. ft.
Elevation C:
Total living space—1129 sq. ft.
All elevations:
3 bedrooms, 1 bath
Plan includes a basement

✔ The family room option and finished lower level are included with plan order.

✔ The living room/dining room combination is great for entertaining or for family gatherings. An optional fireplace is possible in the living room.

✔ The kitchen is conveniently arranged and has the option of a bay window.

✔ The master bedroom includes a walk-in closet. A master bath option is available with the plan order.

✔ Bedroom three could function as a study.

Order each elevation separately. See index for price details. Plan by The Drees Company.

The diagrams presented here constitute only floor plans and elevations. Purchasers are advised to consult their state and local building regulations and a state-certified architect prior to any construction related to these plans.

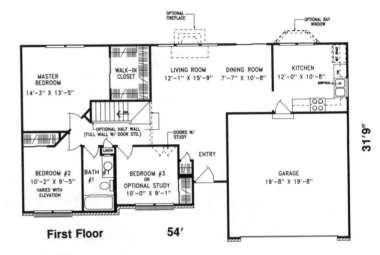

First Floor

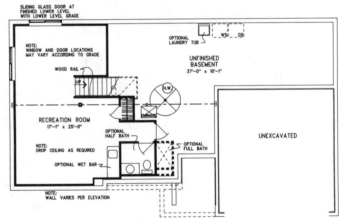

Finished Lower Level

Elevation B: TDC-106B-92DC

Family Room Option

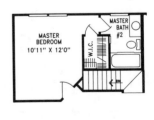

Master Bath Option

Elevation B: TDC-108B-92DC

Elevation C: TDC-108C-92DC

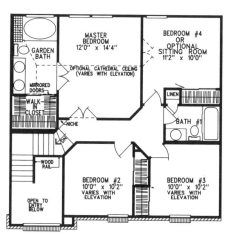

48'

BREAKFAST AREA
9'5" x 9'0"

DISPOSAL DW

KITCHEN
10'0" x 12'8"

ISLAND

RANGE

DINING ROOM
10'6" x 13'0"
WITH DROPPED CEILING

29'

LAUNDRY

PANTRY

DS

OPTIONAL LAUNDRY TUB

REF SPACE

WS

FAMILY ROOM
WITH 10'0" HIGH CEILING
14'1" x 19'6"

DN

BATH #3

LIVING ROOM
15'1" x 12'11"
VARIES WITH ELEVATION

WOOD RAIL

WOOD RAIL

UP

LINE OF FLOOR ABOVE

ENTRY
OPEN TO ABOVE

First Floor

GARDEN BATH

MASTER BEDROOM
12'0" x 14'4"

BEDROOM #4
OR OPTIONAL SITTING ROOM
11'2" x 10'0"

MIRRORED DOORS

OPTIONAL CATHEDRAL CEILING
(VARIES WITH ELEVATION)

LINEN

WALK IN CLOSET

NICHE

DN

BATH #1

WOOD RAIL

BEDROOM #2
10'0" x 10'2"
VARIES WITH ELEVATION

BEDROOM #3
10'0" x 10'2"
VARIES WITH ELEVATION

OPEN TO ENTRY BELOW

Second Floor

The Dominion

Elevation A & C:
First floor—1183 sq. ft.
Second floor—864 sq. ft.
Total living space—2047 sq. ft.

Elevation B:
First floor—1169 sq. ft.
Second floor—861 sq. ft.
Total living space—2030 sq. ft.

All elevations:
4 bedrooms, 2½ baths
Plan includes a basement

✔ The family room features a fireplace and a ten-foot ceiling.

✔ The master bedroom includes a garden bath with a walk-in closet behind mirrored doors.

✔ Bedroom four has the option of being a sitting room off the master bedroom by changing the door placement.

Order each elevation separately. See index for price details. Plan by The Drees Company.

The diagrams presented here constitute only floor plans and elevations. Purchasers are advised to consult their state and local building regulations and a state-certified architect prior to any construction related to these plans.

Elevation A: TDC-108A-92DC

Master Suite Has Double-Door Entry, Private Bath

Total living space—2198 sq. ft.
3 bedrooms, 2 baths
Shown with a basement

✔ The open living area makes this a perfect home for a large family.

✔ The family room and living room share a two-way fireplace.

✔ The island kitchen is handy to the nook and formal dining area.

✔ The nook has access to the covered patio.

✔ The master suite is well separated from the secondary bedrooms.

Plan number AMA-M2495-HS91. See index for pricing details. Plan by Alan Mascord Design Associates.

The diagrams presented here constitute only floor plans and elevations. Purchasers are advised to consult their state and local building regulations and a state-certified architect prior to any construction related to these plans.

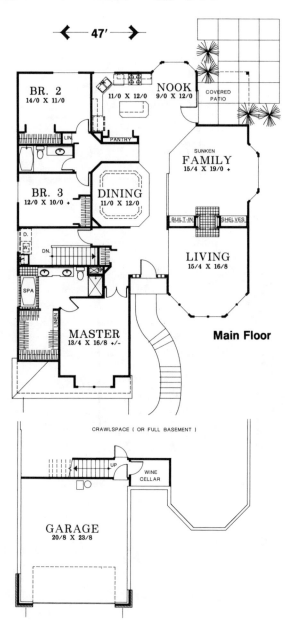

← 47' →

63'

BR. 2
14/0 X 11/0

11/0 X 12/0

NOOK
9/0 X 12/0

COVERED PATIO

LIN

PANTRY

SUNKEN
FAMILY
15/4 X 19/0 +

BR. 3
12/0 X 10/0 +

DINING
11/0 X 12/0

BUILT-IN

SHELVES

D.

W.

DN.

LIVING
15/4 X 16/8

SPA

LINEN

MASTER
13/4 X 16/8 +/-

Main Floor

CRAWLSPACE (OR FULL BASEMENT)

UP

WINE CELLAR

GARAGE
20/8 X 23/8

First Floor

- 32'
- 32'10"
- WOOD DECK
- DINING ROOM 10'-6" x 13'-6"
- KITCHEN
- PANTRY
- DW.
- SINK
- RANGE
- FRIG.
- POWDER
- LIVING ROOM 11'-8" x 14'-2"
- FIREPLACE
- DN
- UP
- COATS
- FOYER
- STUDY 11'-4" x 13'-8"
- COVERED PORCH

Second Floor

- TUB
- MASTER BATH
- BEDROOM #3 11'-2" x 10'-8"
- LINEN
- W.I.C.
- WASH
- DRY
- DN
- MASTER BEDROOM 11'-8" x 14'-2"
- OPEN RAIL
- BATH
- BEDROOM #2 11'-2" x 11'-4"

Study Provides First-Floor Retreat, Office

First floor—816 sq. ft.
Second floor—816 sq. ft.
Total living space—1632 sq. ft.
3 bedrooms, 2½ baths
Shown with a basement

- ✔ Covered front porch accents two story's front elevation, creating a protected entry.

- ✔ Foyer includes a coat closet.

- ✔ Fireplace serves as a focal point in the living room.

- ✔ Swinging patio door in the dining room offers outdoor access.

- ✔ Master bedroom has its own bath and a walk-in closet.

Plan number TNG-396-SU93. See index for price details. Plan by The Norris Group Inc.

The diagrams presented here constitute only floor plans and elevations. Purchasers are advised to consult their state and local building regulations and a state-certified architect prior to any construction related to these plans.

HILDENBRANDT

Modern Exterior Belies
Comfortable Spaciousness

First floor—2178 sq. ft.
Second floor—1297 sq. ft.
Total living space—3475 sq. ft.
3 bedrooms, 2½ baths
Shown with a basement

- Large master bedroom/bath suite includes spa and compartmented toilet. Walk-in closet has built-in "tipdown" ironing board.

- Island kitchen offers views into two-story nook and family room.

- Abundant closet spaces are featured in secondary bedrooms, as well as in the den.

- Each of the three bedrooms on the second floor have their own private bathing areas.

- Home has large covered front porch. Master suite also have private porch area.

Plan number AMA-L2486-HS91. See index for pricing details. Plan by Alan Mascord Design Associates.

The diagrams presented here constitute only floor plans and elevations. Purchasers are advised to consult their state and local building regulations and a state-certified architect prior to any construction related to these plans.

First Floor

Second Floor

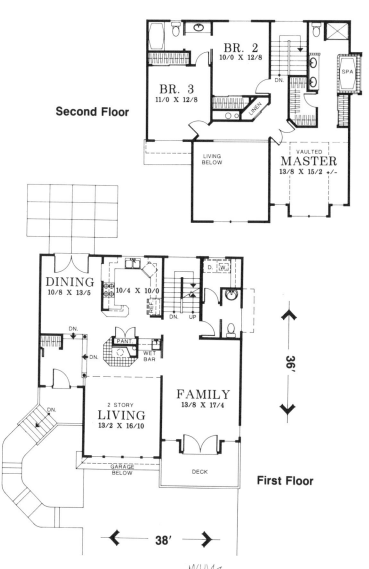

Second Floor

BR. 2
10/0 X 12/8

BR. 3
11/0 X 12/8

SPA

LINEN

LIVING BELOW

VAULTED
MASTER
13/8 X 15/2 +/-

DINING
10/8 X 13/5

D. W.

10/4 X 10/0

REF.

DN. UP

PANT.

WET BAR

DN.

FAMILY
13/8 X 17/4

2 STORY
LIVING
13/2 X 16/10

GARAGE BELOW

DECK

36'

38'

First Floor

Stacked Windows Highlight Contemporary Exterior

First floor—1137 sq. ft.
Second floor—943 sq. ft.
Total living space—2080 sq. ft.
3 bedrooms, 2½ baths
Shown with a basement

✔ The living room includes a fireplace and a wet bar.

✔ The dining room has access to the rear patio.

✔ The family room has French-door access to a balcony.

✔ Upstairs, the master suite includes two closets and a large bath with a separate shower and spa tub.

✔ Bedrooms two and three each have private access to a shared bath.

Plan number AMA-M2411-8907. See index for pricing details. Plan by Alan Mascord Design Associates.

The diagrams presented here constitute only floor plans and elevations. Purchasers are advised to consult their state and local building regulations and a state-certified architect prior to any construction related to these plans.

Cozy Plan Makes Efficient Use Of Space

Total living space—1693 sq. ft.
4 bedrooms, 2 baths
Shown with a basement

✔ A modest-sized porch leads to the formal entry. From the entry visitors see the great room with its welcoming fireplace and the formal dining room to the right of the entry.

✔ There is access to the kitchen from both the dining and living rooms. A flight of stairs leads to the basement, laundry area and the garage nestled under the house.

✔ The kitchen features plentry of storage. A window over the sink faces the front yard. The breakfast area cozies up to a bay window that overlooks the back deck.

✔ Three secondary bedrooms have ample closet space. One of the bedrooms has a built-in desk nook. The two bedrooms facing the front of the house also have window seats.

Plan number CCI-2692-AJ92. See index for pricing details. Plan by Custom Creations Inc.

The diagrams presented here constitute only floor plans and elevations. Purchasers are advised to consult their state and local building regulations and a state-certified architect prior to any construction related to these plans.

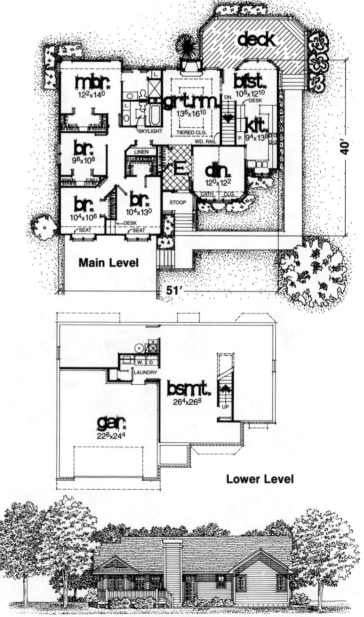

Main Level

Lower Level

Rear Elevation

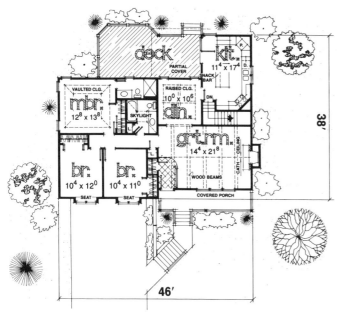

Main floor

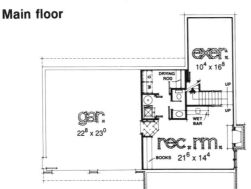

Lower level

Country Classic Provides A Cozy Refuge For The Growing Family

**Total living space—1376 sq. ft.
3 bedrooms, 2 baths, ½ optional
Shown with a basement (582 sq. ft.)**

- The covered porch is perfect for enjoying summer evenings.

- The centralized great room, with volume ceiling and fireplace, is a natural gathering place for the family.

- The kitchen includes an abundance of features that would please any cook.

- Endless hours of outdoor living could be spent on the oversized rear deck.

- The luxurious master suite is accented by a vaulted ceiling and a compartmented bath.

Plan number CCI-2512-9010. See index for pricing details. Plan by Custom Creations Inc.

The diagrams presented here constitute only floor plans and elevations. Purchasers are advised to consult their state and local building regulations and a state-certified architect prior to any construction related to these plans.

Plan Provides Double Bonus: Extra Rooms On Upper Floor

First floor—2046 sq. ft.
Second floor—651 sq. ft.
Total living space—2697 sq. ft.
3 bedrooms, 3 baths
Shown with a basement

- ✔ Entry offers see-through clearance to the family room.

- ✔ First-floor bedrooms make for easy living.

- ✔ Two bonus rooms on the upper floor may be used for hobbies, exercise, entertainment or as extra bedrooms.

- ✔ Plan is designed for lots that rise up from the street approximately 8'.

- ✔ Family room has a vaulted ceiling, a fireplace and built-in shelves.

Plan number AMA-M2486-AJ91. See index for pricing details. Plan by Alan Mascord Design Associates.

The diagrams presented here constitute only floor plans and elevations. Purchasers are advised to consult their state and local building regulations and a state-certified architect prior to any construction related to these plans.

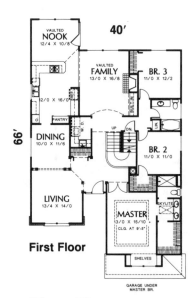

First Floor

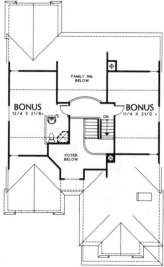

Second Floor

Second Floor

43'

61'

First Floor

Formal Entry Is
Flanked By Living Room
And Dining Room

First floor—1766 sq. ft.
Second floor—1124 sq. ft.
Total living space—2890 sq. ft.
3-4 bedrooms, 3 baths
Shown with a basement

✔ This plan is designed to handle a slope
of 10 to 12 feet in the depth of the home.

✔ The U-shaped kitchen is handy to the
dining room and breakfast nook.

✔ The family room and the living room
each have a fireplace.

✔ The main-floor den could be used as a
bedroom.

✔ Upstairs, the master suite has a private
deck, walk-in closet and a private bath
with separate shower and spa tub.

**Plan number AMA-2417-89MO. See
index for pricing details. Plan by Alan
Mascord Design Associates.**

The diagrams presented here constitute only floor plans
and elevations. Purchasers are advised to consult their
state and local building regulations and a state-certified
architect prior to any construction related to these plans.

Custom Staircase Heightens Entry Excitement

First floor—1112 sq. ft.
Second floor—1164 sq. ft.
Total living space—2276 sq. ft.
4 bedrooms, 2½ baths
Shown with a basement

- ✔ Sculptural staircase creates a dramatic focal point in the foyer.

- ✔ Custom ceiling treatments, including a cathedral ceiling in the entry, enhance the interior.

- ✔ Kitchen, breakfast area and family room share views in an open floor plan.

- ✔ Oversized master bedroom includes two walk-in closets and an amenity-packed bath.

- ✔ Second-floor balcony offers a view into the family room.

Plan number TCB-1294-SU93. See index for price details. Plan by Barton & Associates, Inc.

The diagrams presented here constitute only floor plans and elevations. Purchasers are advised to consult their state and local building regulations and a state-certified architect prior to any construction related to these plans.

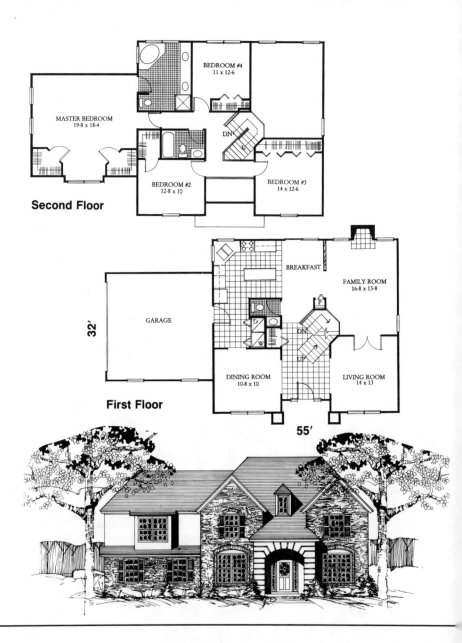

Covered Porch Affords A Warm Welcome

First floor—1076 sq. ft.
Second floor—781 sq. ft.
Total living space—1857 sq. ft.
3 bedrooms, 2½ baths
Shown with a basement

- ✔ Formal dining room adjoins the spacious living room.

- ✔ Attractive, corner sink serves as a bright work area in the kitchen.

- ✔ Family room features a fireplace focal point.

- ✔ Two linen closets offer generous storage space for sheets and towels.

First Floor

Second Floor

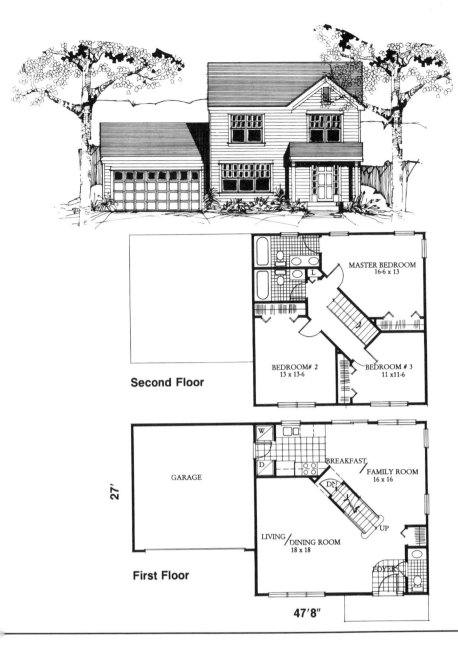

Second Floor

MASTER BEDROOM
16-6 x 13

BEDROOM# 2
13 x 13-6

BEDROOM # 3
11 x11-6

First Floor

GARAGE

BREAKFAST

FAMILY ROOM
16 x 16

DN

UP

LIVING / DINING ROOM
18 x 18

FOYER

27'

47'8"

Combined Space Maximizes Impact Of Living, Dining Rooms

First floor—756 sq. ft.
Second floor—729 sq. ft.
Total living space—1485 sq. ft.
3 bedrooms, 2½ baths
Shown with a basement

✔ By sharing visual space, the living and dining rooms appear to be larger than they actually are.

✔ Attractive, open railing highlights the central staircase.

✔ Handy breakfast area provides informal dining space adjoining the kitchen.

✔ Dual-basin vanity enhances the master bath.

✔ Both secondary bedrooms are spacious and comfortable.

Plan number TCB-1295-SU93. See index for price details. Plan by Barton & Associates, Inc.

The diagrams presented here constitute only floor plans and elevations. Purchasers are advised to consult their state and local building regulations and a state-certified architect prior to any construction related to these plans.

✔ Walk-in closet is a plus in the master suite which also has a full bath.

✔ Sliding glass doors in the breakfast area offer outdoor access.

✔ Laundry room doubles as a handy mud room entry.

✔ Main-floor powder room includes a window.

Plan number TCB-1296-SU93. See index for price details. Plan by Barton & Associates, Inc.

The diagrams presented here constitute only floor plans and elevations. Purchasers are advised to consult their state and local building regulations and a state-certified architect prior to any construction related to these plans.

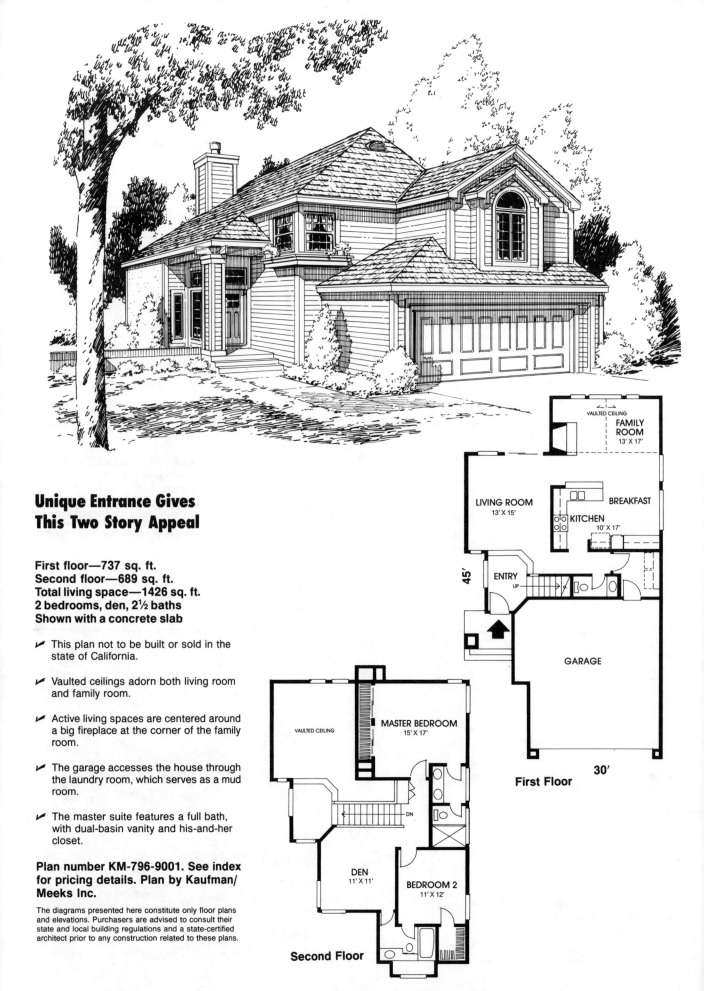

Unique Entrance Gives
This Two Story Appeal

First floor—737 sq. ft.
Second floor—689 sq. ft.
Total living space—1426 sq. ft.
2 bedrooms, den, 2½ baths
Shown with a concrete slab

✔ This plan not to be built or sold in the state of California.

✔ Vaulted ceilings adorn both living room and family room.

✔ Active living spaces are centered around a big fireplace at the corner of the family room.

✔ The garage accesses the house through the laundry room, which serves as a mud room.

✔ The master suite features a full bath, with dual-basin vanity and his-and-her closet.

Plan number KM-796-9001. See index for pricing details. Plan by Kaufman/Meeks Inc.

The diagrams presented here constitute only floor plans and elevations. Purchasers are advised to consult their state and local building regulations and a state-certified architect prior to any construction related to these plans.

VAULTED CEILING
FAMILY ROOM
13' X 17'

LIVING ROOM
13' X 15'

BREAKFAST

KITCHEN
10' X 17'

ENTRY
UP

45'

GARAGE

30'

First Floor

MASTER BEDROOM
15' X 17'

VAULTED CEILING

DN

DEN
11' X 11'

BEDROOM 2
11' X 12'

Second Floor

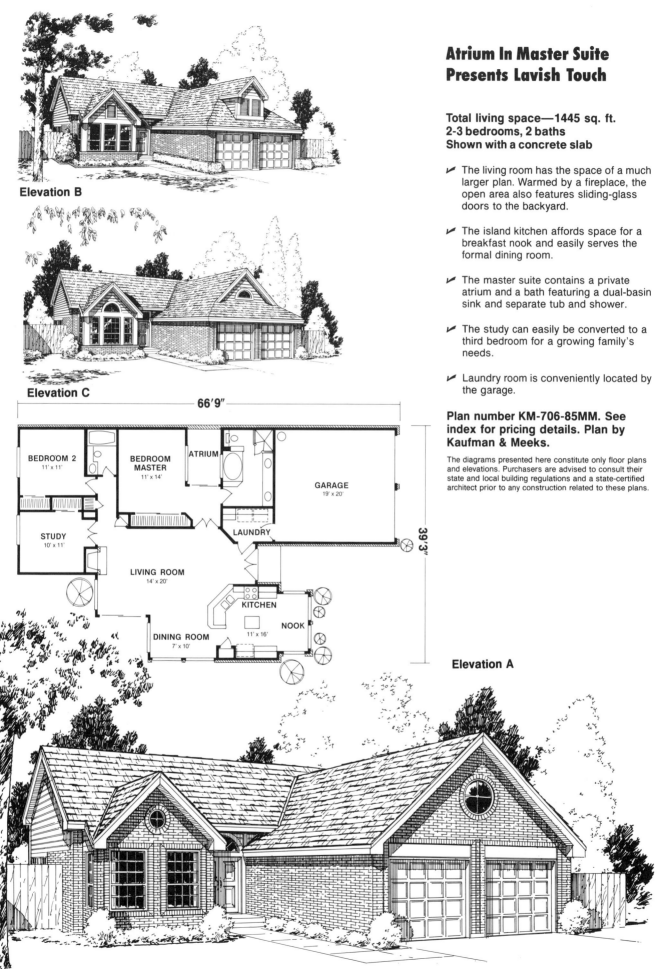

Elevation B

Elevation C

Atrium In Master Suite Presents Lavish Touch

Total living space—1445 sq. ft.
2-3 bedrooms, 2 baths
Shown with a concrete slab

✔ The living room has the space of a much larger plan. Warmed by a fireplace, the open area also features sliding-glass doors to the backyard.

✔ The island kitchen affords space for a breakfast nook and easily serves the formal dining room.

✔ The master suite contains a private atrium and a bath featuring a dual-basin sink and separate tub and shower.

✔ The study can easily be converted to a third bedroom for a growing family's needs.

✔ Laundry room is conveniently located by the garage.

Plan number KM-706-85MM. See index for pricing details. Plan by Kaufman & Meeks.

The diagrams presented here constitute only floor plans and elevations. Purchasers are advised to consult their state and local building regulations and a state-certified architect prior to any construction related to these plans.

66'9"

BEDROOM 2
11' x 11'

BEDROOM MASTER
11' x 14'

ATRIUM

GARAGE
19' x 20'

STUDY
10' x 11'

LAUNDRY

LIVING ROOM
14' x 20'

39'3"

KITCHEN
11' x 16'

NOOK

DINING ROOM
7' x 10'

Elevation A

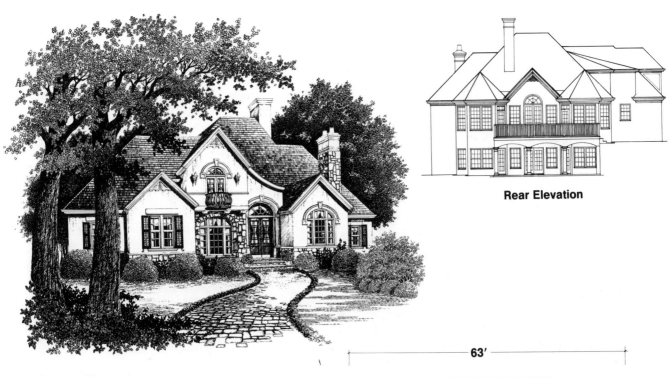

Rear Elevation

Second-Floor Balcony Gives French-Style Home Curb Appeal

First floor—1900 sq. ft.
Second floor—800 sq. ft.
Total living space—2700 sq. ft.
4 bedrooms, 2½ baths
Shown with a basement

- ✔ From the foyer, visitors have dramatic view of great room.

- ✔ Great room and study each have a fireplace.

- ✔ The first-floor master suite is a luxury enclave. Bedroom has tray ceiling and access to the rear deck. Bath includes two walk-in closets, separate tub and shower, his-and-her vanities and a compartmented toilet.

- ✔ Large island kitchen is handy to the breakfast and dining room.

- ✔ A pocket door separates the laundry room from the kitchen.

Plan number DTA-M2609-DT91. See index for pricing details. Plan by Design Traditions Atlanta.

The diagrams presented here constitute only floor plans and elevations. Purchasers are advised to consult their state and local building regulations and a state-certified architect prior to any construction related to these plans.

First Floor

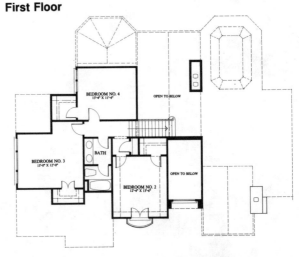

Second Floor

Rear Elevation

First Floor

69'5"

74'6"

Second Floor

Breezeway Attaches Garage To House

First floor—1960 sq. ft.
Second floor—905 sq. ft.
Total living space—2865 sq. ft.
4 bedrooms, 2½ baths
Plan includes a basement

- Island kitchen is handy to the breakfast room and dining room.

- Two-story great room is prefect for entertaining.

- Master suite includes gigantic walk-in closet and bath with oval tub, his-and-her vanities and compartmented toilet.

- Living and great room each have a fireplace.

- Upstairs, bedroom two has a private bath. Bedrooms three and four share a large, compartmented bath.

Plan number DTA-L2612-DT91. See index for pricing details. Plan by Design Traditions.

The diagrams presented here constitute only floor plans and elevations. Purchasers are advised to consult their state and local building regulations and a state-certified architect prior to any construction related to these plans.

Multilevel Home Has Large Windows To Catch The Sun

First floor—1316 sq. ft.
Second floor—592 sq. ft.
Total living space—1908 sq. ft.
3 bedrooms, 2 baths
Plan includes a crawl space/pilings or basement

✔ The living room, with sloped ceiling, includes a fireplace.

✔ The dining room is open to the island kitchen.

✔ Bedrooms two and three have large closets and share a compartmented hall bath.

✔ Upstairs, the very private master suite has a sloped ceiling, balcony and large walk-in closet. Master bath has a compartmented toilet, his-and-her vanity and an oval tub.

Plan number TGC-M593-HS91. See index for pricing details. Plan by The Garlinghouse Co.

The diagrams presented here constitute only floor plans and elevations. Purchasers are advised to consult their state and local building regulations and a state-certified architect prior to any construction related to these plans.

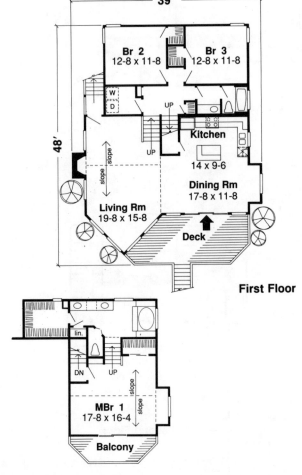

39'

48'

Br 2
12-8 x 11-8

Br 3
12-8 x 11-8

W
D

UP

Kitchen

UP

14 x 9-6

Dining Rm
17-8 x 11-8

Living Rm
19-8 x 15-8

Deck

First Floor

lin.

DN   UP

MBr 1
17-8 x 16-4

Balcony

Second Floor

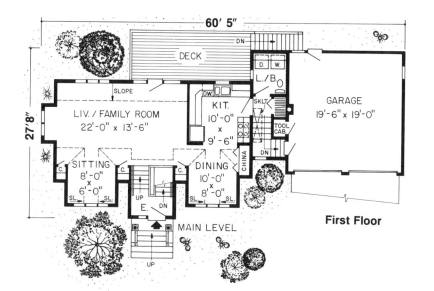

60' 5"

27' 8"

DECK

DN

D. | W.

L./B.

DW.

KIT.
10'-0"
x
9'-6"

SKLT.

TOOL CAB.

GARAGE
19'-6" x 19'-0"

SLOPE

LIV. / FAMILY ROOM
22'-0" x 13'-6"

CHINA

DN

SITTING
8'-0"
x
6'-0"

C.

C.

DINING
10'-0"
x
8'-0"

SL.

SL.

SL.

SL.

UP

E.

DN

UP

MAIN LEVEL

First Floor

PATIO

UP

U.

GARAGE

M. BEDRM.
12'-4" x 13'-2"

LIN.

B.

W.H.

F.

COUNTER

SEAT

UP

B.

UP

BEDRM. 3
10'-0"
x
10'-0"

C.

BEDRM. 2
10'-0"
x
10'-0"

Lower Level

Traditional Touches
Adorn Compact Design

First floor—668 sq. ft.
Lower floor—764 sq. ft.
Total living space—1432 sq. ft.
3 bedrooms, 2 baths
Plan includes a concrete slab

- Unusual ceiling treatments add interest to public areas.

- A rear deck takes in views.

- The kitchen is open to the dining room. The dining room has a built-in china cabinet.

- The utility room also serves as a ¼ bath.

- Downstairs, the master bedroom includes a large walk-in closet and a bath with separate tub and shower, and double-bowled vanity.

- Bedrooms two and three share a hall bath.

Plan number TGC-599-HS91. See index for pricing details. Plan by The Garlinghouse Co.

The diagrams presented here constitute only floor plans and elevations. Purchasers are advised to consult their state and local building regulations and a state-certified architect prior to any construction related to these plans.

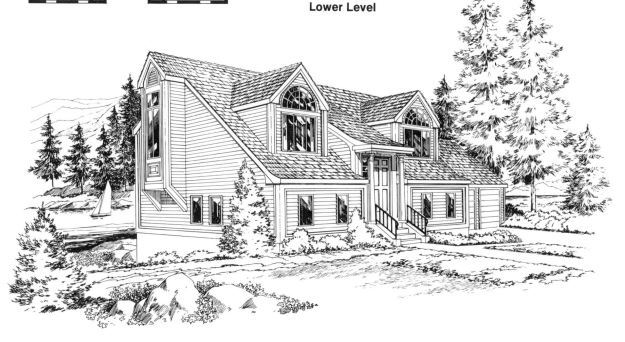

Second-Floor Expansion Space Is An Exciting Option

First floor—1130 sq. ft.
Second floor—370 sq. ft.
Total living space—1500 sq. ft.
3 bedrooms, 2½ baths
Shown with a basement

- An angled powder room and a coat closet are included in the foyer for entry convenience.

- A plant ledge accents the division of space between the living and dining rooms.

- The living room features floor-to-ceiling windows alongside the fireplace.

- A private patio extends the space of the master suite.

Plan number RFF-2112-8903. See index for pricing details. Plan by Fillmore Design Group.

The diagrams presented here constitute only floor plans and elevations. Purchasers are advised to consult their state and local building regulations and a state-certified architect prior to any construction related to these plans.

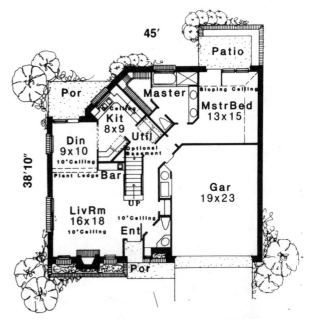

First Floor

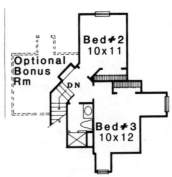

Second Floor

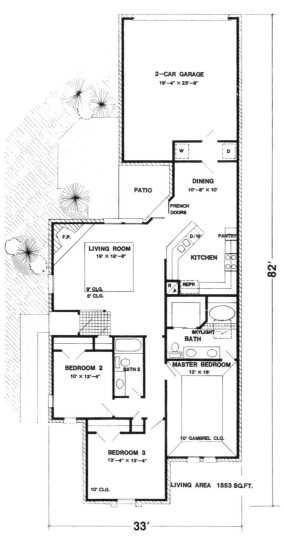

French Manor

Total living space— 1553 sq. ft.
3 bedrooms, 2 baths
Shown with a concrete slab

✔ Living room features a 9-foot step-up ceiling, raised hearth corner fireplace & side entry.

✔ French doors between the living and dining areas open onto a private patio, providing natural light and views for the kitchen.

✔ The master suite has a 10-foot gambrel ceiling, and skylit master bath with Roman tub, walk-in closet, and double-bowl vanity.

✔ Two additional bedrooms, one with a 10-foot ceiling, share a hall bath.

✔ The contemporary French exterior features a rear-loaded garage.

Plan number LWG-1010-87ZZ. See index for pricing details. Plan by Larry W. Garnett & Associates.

The diagrams presented here constitute only floor plans and elevations. Purchasers are advised to consult their state and local building regulations and a state-certified architect prior to any construction related to these plans.

Vaulted Spaces And Open Stairway Say 'Welcome'

First floor—702 sq. ft.
Second floor—396 sq. ft.
Total living space—1098 sq. ft.
3 bedrooms, 2 baths
Shown with a crawlspace

✔ A covered front porch protects the entry to this two-story home.

✔ Great room shares the warmth of its fireplace with the dining room and kitchen.

✔ A patio door offers easy outside access.

✔ Main-floor master bedroom has a walk-in closet. A central full bath serves this room and the living areas.

✔ Two bedrooms and a full bath complete the second floor.

Plan number HR-689-88MM. See index for pricing details. Plan by Historical Replications Inc.

The diagrams presented here constitute only floor plans and elevations. Purchasers are advised to consult their state and local building regulations and a state-certified architect prior to any construction related to these plans.

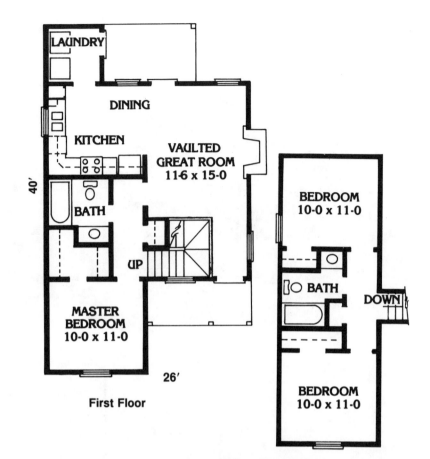

First Floor

Second Floor

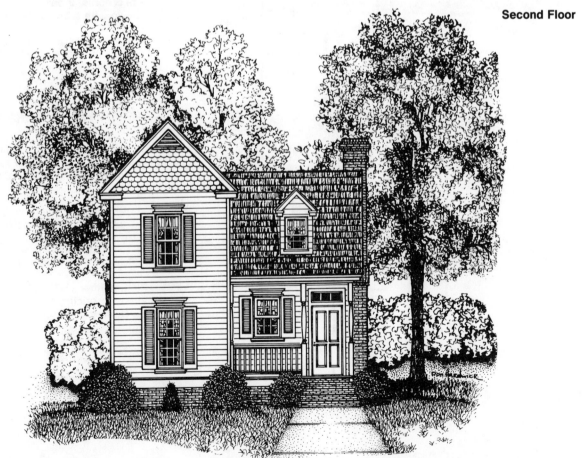

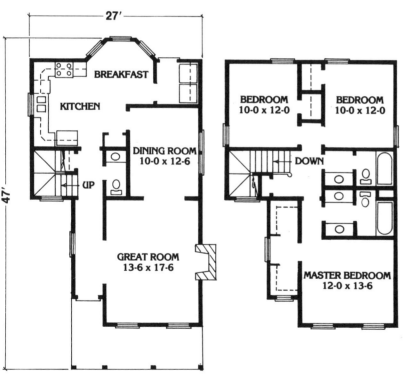

First Floor

Second Floor

Great Room, With Fireplace, Provides A Warm Welcome

First floor—846 sq. ft.
Second floor—784 sq. ft.
Total living space—1630 sq. ft.
3 bedrooms, 2½ baths
Shown with a crawlspace

✔ Farmhouse-style exterior features a covered porch, divided-sash windows and fish scale accents.

✔ Central powder room is also convenient to the foyer.

✔ Breakfast bay provides informal dining space in the kitchen.

✔ Separate dining room provides entertaining space for special occasions.

✔ Utility room serves as mud room entry from the backyard.

Plan number HR-601-8808. See index for pricing details. Plan by Historical Replications Inc.

The diagrams presented here constitute only floor plans and elevations. Purchasers are advised to consult their state and local building regulations and a state-certified architect prior to any construction related to these plans.

Colonial Penrose Promises Classic Living To A Growing Family

First floor—1004 sq. ft.
Second floor—986 sq. ft.
Total living space—1990 sq. ft.
3 bedrooms, 2½ baths
Plan includes a basement

- A garden whirlpool, dual-basin vanity, plant ledge, walk-in closet and a vaulted ceiling complement the master suite.

- The tiered ceiling adds elegance to the dining room.

- Laundry facilities are carefully placed on the second floor near the bedrooms.

- The breakfast area has access to the deck.

- The family room is warmed by a fireplace and opens to the wood deck.

Plan number CCI-M2609-9107. See index for pricing details. Plan by Custom Creations Inc.

The diagrams presented here constitute only floor plans and elevations. Purchasers are advised to consult their state and local building regulations and a state-certified architect prior to any construction related to these plans.

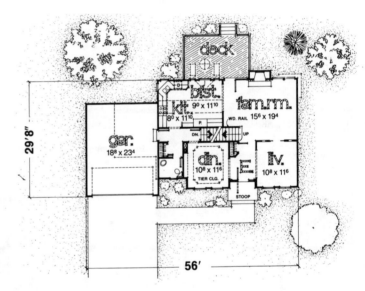

First Floor

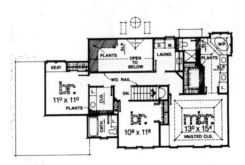

Second Floor

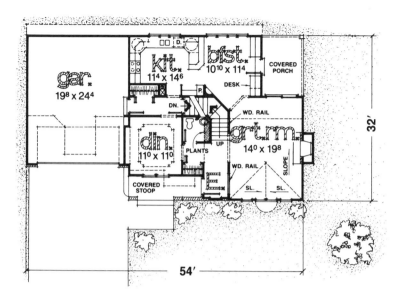

First Floor

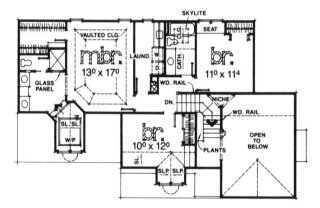

Second Floor

The Finsbury Adds New Life To The Traditional Two Story

First floor—1028 sq. ft.
Second floor—1008 sq. ft.
Total living space—2036 sq. ft.
3 bedrooms, 2½ baths
Plan includes a basement

- Great room highlights include a fireplace, an innovative sloped ceiling and wood railings.

- The breakfast and great rooms have access to the covered porch.

- Privacy can be found in the master suite, which includes a vaulted ceiling, walk-in closet and a separate, windowed whirlpool area.

- Laundry facilities are conveniently located near bedrooms on the second floor.

- Plant shelf brings life to the entryway.

- A skylight is included with the main bath on the second floor.

Plan number CCI-M2608-9107. See index for pricing details. Plan by Custom Creations Inc.

The diagrams presented here constitute only floor plans and elevations. Purchasers are advised to consult their state and local building regulations and a state-certified architect prior to any construction related to these plans.

Rear Elevation

Walk-Out Basement Suits
Sloped Lot

First floor—1678 sq. ft.
Second floor—1677 sq. ft.
Total living space—3355 sq. ft.
4 bedrooms, 3½ baths
Plan includes a basement

- ✔ The first-floor guest room with full bath would suit an in-law arrangement or could be used as maid's quarters.

- ✔ The living room has a vaulted ceiling.

- ✔ The dining room has a bay window.

- ✔ The family room includes a fireplace and French-door access to a rear deck.

- ✔ Upstairs, the master suite includes a large study with built-in bookcases. The bedroom includes a fireplace. The bath has an oval tub set in a bay window.

- ✔ Bedrooms three and four share a compartmented bath. Bedroom three has a huge walk-in closet.

Plan number DTA-L2619-DT91. See index for pricing details. Plan by Design Traditions.

The diagrams presented here constitute only floor plans and elevations. Purchasers are advised to consult their state and local building regulations and a state-certified architect prior to any construction related to these plans.

First Floor

Second Floor

Code: DIFF

To Order, Phone Toll Free 1-800-323-7379

Storage Area Doubles As Workshop

Total living space—1725 sq. ft.
3 bedrooms, 2 baths
Shown on a basement

✔ Formal dining room off the foyer is open to the great room, which has a fireplace, bay windows and access to the rear deck.

✔ Master bedroom has a tray ceiling. The master bath has a walk-in closet, two vanities, tub and separate shower, and toilet compartment.

✔ A full bath serves bedrooms two and three, both equipped with deep closets.

✔ Laundry room is conveniently located near all bedrooms.

Plan number DTA-2597-AJ92. See index for pricing details. Plan by Design Traditions.

The diagrams presented here constitute only floor plans and elevations. Purchasers are advised to consult their state and local building regulations and a state-certified architect prior to any construction related to these plans.

Main Level

Lower Level

Creative Floor Plan
Will Suit Growing Families

First floor—1453 sq. ft.
Second floor—1016 sq. ft.
Bonus room—251 sq. ft.
Total living space—2720 sq. ft.
3 bedrooms, den, 2½ baths
Shown with basement

- Plan is designed for lots sloping up approximately 8′ in depth of home.

- Master-suite spa is situated beneath a bay window for cozy comfort.

- Bonus room can serve as an extra bedroom, a hobby center, an exercise area or another den.

- Island kitchen includes a planning desk and a pantry.

- A decorative railing separates the one-and-a-half-story living room from the dining room.

- Varied roof pitches provide exterior interest to this home.

- Windows with true-divided lights decorate the interior and exterior.

Plan number AMA-M2491-HS91. See index for pricing details. Plan by Alan Mascord Design Associates.

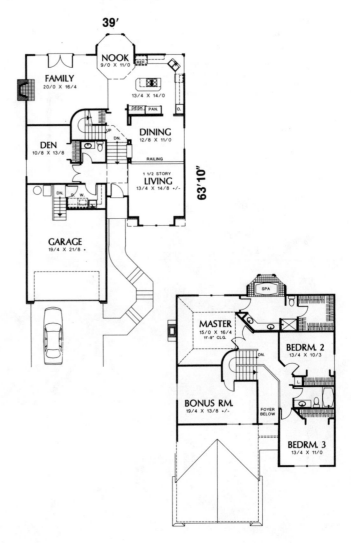

The diagrams presented here constitute only floor plans and elevations. Purchasers are advised to consult their state and local building regulations and a state-certified architect prior to any construction related to these plans.

Master Suite Is Owners' Retreat

First floor—2177 sq. ft.
Lower floor—1752 sq. ft.
Total living space—3929 sq. ft.
3 bedrooms, 2½ baths
Office and den

✔ The open living area is perfect for entertaining.

✔ The family area is perfect for quiet evenings at home. The island kitchen allows the cook to enjoy activity in the family room.

✔ The family room and the living room each have a fireplace.

✔ The first-floor master suite includes a private deck, luxury bath and a huge closet/dressing room.

✔ Downstairs, the game room with walk-in wet bar is a great party room.

✔ The den and home office each have access to the rear deck.

✔ The secondary bedrooms share a compartmented hall bath.

Plan number AMA-2496-HS91. See index for pricing details. Plan by Alan Mascord Design Associates.

The diagrams presented here constitute only floor plans and elevations. Purchasers are advised to consult their state and local building regulations and a state-certified architect prior to any construction related to these plans.

Rear Elevation

Neo-Traditional House Fits On Narrow Lot

First floor—877 sq. ft.
Second floor—323 sq. ft.
Total living space—1200 sq. ft.
2 bedrooms, 2 baths
Shown with a crawlspace

✔ The spacious great room joins the dining area to provide space for large gatherings.

✔ The U-shaped kitchen provides plenty of counter space.

✔ The master suite has a walk-in closet and a bath.

✔ The second bedroom also has a walk-in closet and a bath.

✔ A large attic can be used for storage space.

Plan number RJA-2200-91ZZ. See index for pricing details. Plan by Ralph Jones & Associates.

The diagrams presented here constitute only floor plans and elevations. Purchasers are advised to consult their state and local building regulations and a state-certified architect prior to any construction related to these plans.

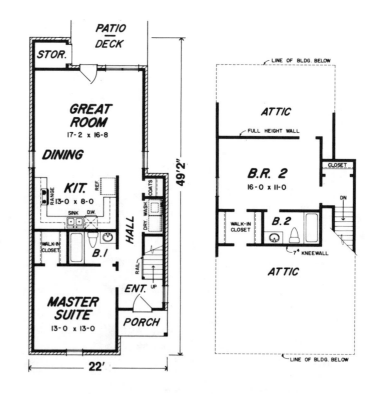

First Floor   **Second Floor**

Rear Elevation

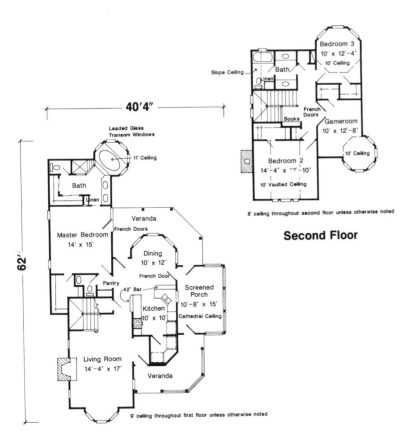

First Floor

40'4"

62'

Leaded Glass
Transom Windows

11' Ceiling

Bath

Linen

Veranda

Master Bedroom
14' x 15'

French Doors

Dining
10' x 12'

French Door

Pantry

42' Bar

Screened
Porch
10'-8" x 15'

Kitchen
10' x 10'

Cathedral Ceiling

Living Room
14'-4" x 17'

Veranda

9' ceiling throughout first floor unless otherwise noted

Second Floor

Slope Ceiling

Bath

Linen

Books

Bedroom 3
10' x 12'-4"
10' Ceiling

French
Doors

Gameroom
10' x 12'-8"

Bedroom 2
14'-4" x 12'-10"

10' Vaulted Ceiling

10' Ceiling

8' ceiling throughout second floor unless otherwise noted

Twin Verandas Add Character, Front And Back Views

First floor—1236 sq. ft.
Second floor—835 sq. ft.
Total living space—2071 sq. ft.
3 bedrooms, 2½ baths
Shown with a concrete slab

- ✔ Generous use of custom window treatments customize and brighten the interior.

- ✔ Cathedral ceiling highlights the screened porch.

- ✔ Second-floor game room includes a walk-in closet and a separate sitting area.

- ✔ Plans for a detached two-car garage are included.

Plan number LWG-1099-SU93. See index for price details. Plan by Larry W. Garnett & Associates Inc.

The diagrams presented here constitute only floor plans and elevations. Purchasers are advised to consult their state and local building regulations and a state-certified architect prior to any construction related to these plans.

Plan number KM-707-90MJ

Second Floor

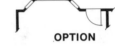

OPTION

Impressive Entry Opens To Gracious Formal Living Spaces

First floor—1052 sq. ft.
Second floor—1040 sq. ft.
Total living space—2092 sq. ft.
4 bedrooms, 2½ baths
Shown with a basement

✔ The two-story entry is flanked by the living room and dining room.

✔ Sunken family room will be a favorite gathering spot complete with fireplace and access to the kitchen and outdoors.

✔ The island kitchen has plenty of counter space for easy meal preparation and opens up to the sunny breakfast area with bay window.

✔ The master suite, located on the second floor, features two large closets and a private bath with double vanity.

✔ All secondary bedrooms include generous closet space and share a hall bath.

Please order each elevation separately. See index for pricing details. Plan by Kaufman/Meeks Inc.

The diagrams presented here constitute only floor plans and elevations. Purchasers are advised to consult their state and local building regulations and a state-certified architect prior to any construction related to these plans.

First Floor

Plan number KM-708-90MJ

Plan number KM-709-90MJ

Secondary Bedrooms Are Functional, Versatile, Will Suit A Variety Of Needs

First floor—1070 sq. ft.
Second floor—480 sq. ft.
Total living space—1550 sq. ft.
2-3 bedrooms, 2 baths
Shown with a concrete slab or basement

- Main-floor bedroom has its own access to a compartmented bath. Double-door entry gives it appeal as a study.

- Adaptable room upstairs may serve as a nursery, bedroom or master sitting area.

- Handy pass-through connects the kitchen and living room.

- Bay window expands rear view, brightens dining room.

- Each order includes all elevations shown.

Plan number KM-702-85MM. See index for pricing details. Plan by Kaufman/Meeks Inc.

The diagrams presented here constitute only floor plans and elevations. Purchasers are advised to consult their state and local building regulations and a state-certified architect prior to any construction related to these plans.

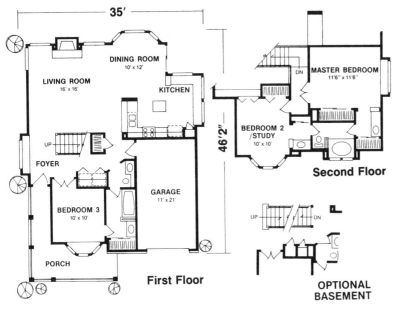

35'

46'2"

DINING ROOM
10' x 12'

LIVING ROOM
16' x 16'

KITCHEN

FOYER

UP

GARAGE
11' x 21'

BEDROOM 3
10' x 10'

PORCH

First Floor

MASTER BEDROOM
11'6" x 11'6"

DN

BEDROOM 2
/STUDY
10' x 10'

Second Floor

UP   DN

OPTIONAL BASEMENT

Charming Home Delivers
A Facade Nostalgic
Of An Earlier Era

First floor—846 sq. ft.
Second floor—784 sq. ft.
Total living space—1630 sq. ft.
3 bedrooms, 2½ baths
Shown with a crawlspace

✔ The entry leads into the spacious kitchen and breakfast room. The breakfast room is flooded with light from a bay window.

✔ The great room, located off the entry, is warmed by a fireplace and looks out to the front porch.

✔ The formal dining room is served easily from the kitchen and opens into the great room.

✔ The master bedroom has a large closet and access to a full bath.

✔ A walk-in laundry room is an added convenience.

Plan number HR-601-9104. See index for pricing details. Plan by Historical Replications Inc.

The diagrams presented here constitute only floor plans and elevations. Purchasers are advised to consult their state and local building regulations and a state-certified architect prior to any construction related to these plans.

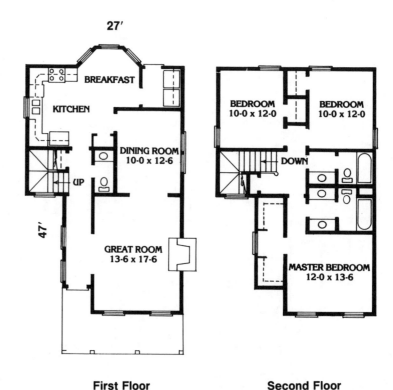

First Floor   **Second Floor**

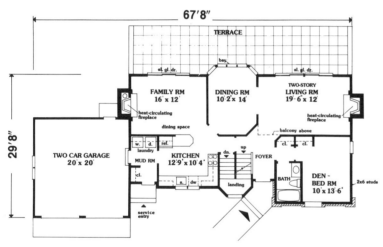

First Floor

Second Floor

This Move Up Has Great Street Appeal

First floor—1201 sq. ft.
Second floor—978 sq. ft.
Total living space—2179 sq. ft.
3-4 bedrooms, 3 baths
Shown with a concrete slab/basement

✔ The second-floor master suite has a bay window, a walk-in closet, a dressing room, dual vanities and a whirlpool tub.

✔ The secondary bedrooms have walk-in closets. Part of the bedroom hall dramatically overlooks the living room.

✔ The first-floor den can be converted into a fourth bedroom.

✔ Both the living room and family room have heat-circulating fireplaces and sliding-glass doors to the terrace. The living room has a two-story ceiling.

✔ The kitchen overlooks the family room and has a snack bar.

Plan number HFL-M2704-9111. See index for pricing details. Plan by Homes For Living Inc.

The diagrams presented here constitute only floor plans and elevations. Purchasers are advised to consult their state and local building regulations and a state-certified architect prior to any construction related to these plans.

Empty-Nester Villa Perfect For Golf Course Community

Total living space—1569 sq. ft.
2 bedrooms, 2 baths
Shown with a concrete slab

- Retiree or empty-nester villa is designed for golf course patio or "zero-lot line" applications.

- Guest bedroom and adjoining bath anticipate visiting family and friends.

- Large closets and luxury kitchen are targeted for discriminating, mature couple.

- Compact plan, ease of construction hold down costs, keep it affordable for buyers on fixed income.

- Judicious use of glass opens view to golf course or other amenities without compromising privacy.

Order each elevation separately. See index for pricing details. Plan by Quincy Johnson & Associates.

The diagrams presented here constitute only floor plans and elevations. Purchasers are advised to consult their state and local building regulations and a state-certified architect prior to any construction related to these plans.

Plan number QJA-1996-AJ92

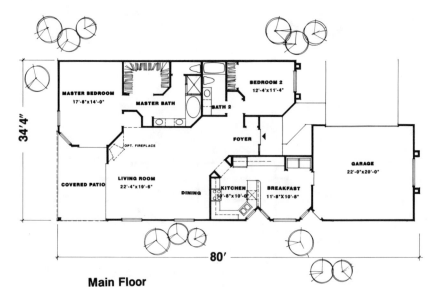

Main Floor

MASTER BEDROOM 17'-8"x14'-0"
MASTER BATH
BATH 2
BEDROOM 2 12'-4"x11'-4"
OPT. FIREPLACE
FOYER
GARAGE 22'-0"x20'-0"
COVERED PATIO
LIVING ROOM 22'-4"x19'-6"
DINING
KITCHEN 10'-8"x10'-0"
BREAKFAST 11'-8"X10'-8"
34'4"
80'

Rear Elevation

Plan number QJA-1995-AJ92

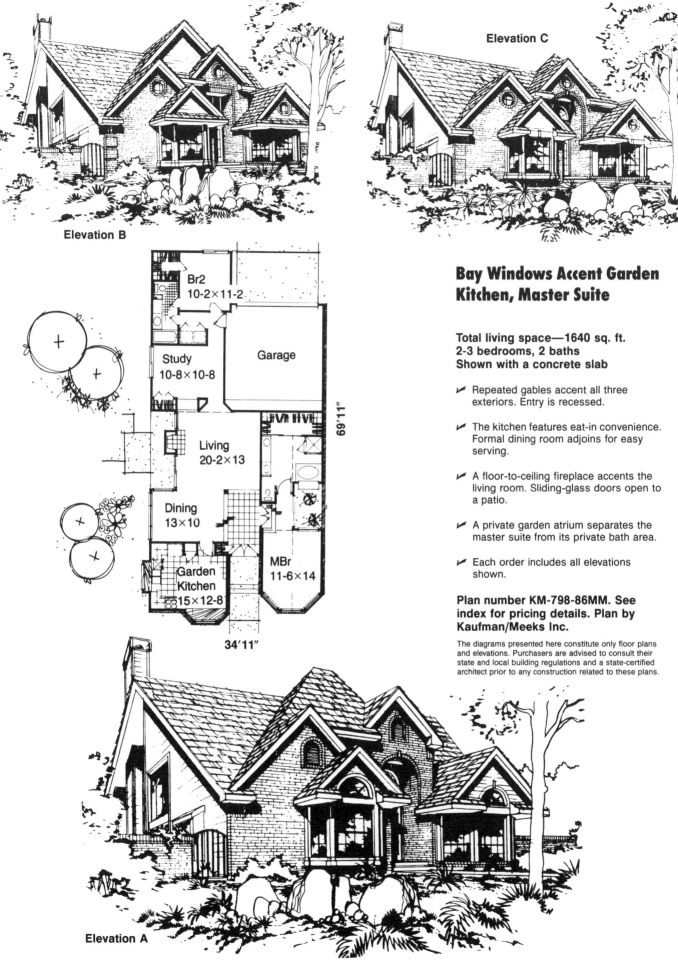

Elevation C

Elevation B

Br2
10-2×11-2

Study
10-8×10-8

Garage

Living
20-2×13

Dining
13×10

Garden
Kitchen
15×12-8

MBr
11-6×14

69'11"

34'11"

Elevation A

Bay Windows Accent Garden Kitchen, Master Suite

**Total living space—1640 sq. ft.
2-3 bedrooms, 2 baths
Shown with a concrete slab**

- Repeated gables accent all three exteriors. Entry is recessed.

- The kitchen features eat-in convenience. Formal dining room adjoins for easy serving.

- A floor-to-ceiling fireplace accents the living room. Sliding-glass doors open to a patio.

- A private garden atrium separates the master suite from its private bath area.

- Each order includes all elevations shown.

Plan number KM-798-86MM. See index for pricing details. Plan by Kaufman/Meeks Inc.

The diagrams presented here constitute only floor plans and elevations. Purchasers are advised to consult their state and local building regulations and a state-certified architect prior to any construction related to these plans.

Colonial Farmhouse Has Modern Amenities

**Total living space—1536 sq. ft.
3 bedrooms, 2½ baths
Shown with a basement**

✔ The family room features a heat-circulating fireplace. Sliding-glass doors access the rear patio.

✔ The kitchen features a closet pantry and an island cooktop, which separates the kitchen from the dinette.

✔ Wood storage niche is provided for the family room fireplace.

✔ Laundry room and mud room is conveniently located off the two-car garage.

Plan number HFL-2705-9202. See index for pricing details. Plan by Homes For Living.

The diagrams presented here constitute only floor plans and elevations. Purchasers are advised to consult their state and local building regulations and a state-certified architect prior to any construction related to these plans.

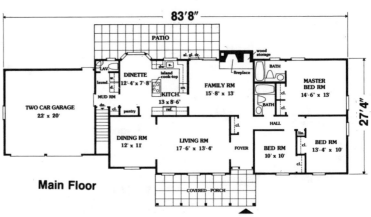

Main Floor

The Traditional One-Story Charlene Is Spacious, Yet Affordable

**Total living space—1476 sq. ft.
3 bedrooms, 2 baths
Optional basement—1361 sq. ft.**

✔ Decorative columns separate the foyer and living room, and the living and dining rooms.

✔ A cathedral ceiling adds to the spaciousness of the living room. The heat-circulating fireplace provides a homey feel.

✔ The dining room's dramatic bow window looks out to the deck.

Plan number HFL-2701-9107. See index for pricing details. Plan by Homes For Living.

The diagrams presented here constitute only floor plans and elevations. Purchasers are advised to consult their state and local building regulations and a state-certified architect prior to any construction related to these plans.

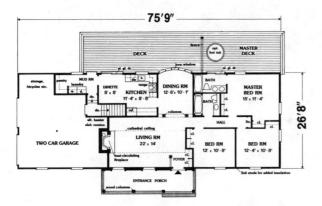

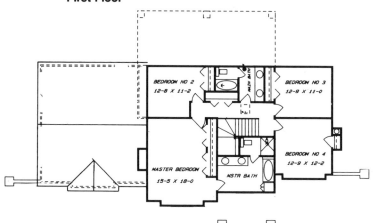

First Floor

Second Floor

Brick Columns Give
Home Colonial Flair

First floor—1198 sq. ft.
Second floor—1191 sq. ft.
Total living space—2389 sq. ft.
4 bedrooms, 2½ baths
Shown with a concrete slab

✔ The formal entry is flanked by the living room and family room.

✔ The living room and dining room configuration is perfect for formal gatherings. The living room has a fireplace.

✔ The large kitchen easily serves the breakfast room and the dining room.

✔ The family room features double-door entry and a fireplace.

✔ Upstairs, the master suite has a luxury bath with compartmented toilet and separate shower and tub.

Plan number DPI-2381-AJ92. See index for pricing details. Plan by Design Profile Inc.

The diagrams presented here constitute only floor plans and elevations. Purchasers are advised to consult their state and local building regulations and a state-certified architect prior to any construction related to these plans.

Extra Living Room Offers Dramatic Rear Views

First floor—810 sq. ft.
Second floor—719 sq. ft.
Total living space—1529 sq. ft.
3 bedrooms, 2½ baths
Shown with a concrete slab

✔ The living room includes a volume ceiling and extends into a functional corner seating alcove. The room also features a fireplace.

✔ The dining room and the breakfast nook are easily served by the centralized kitchen.

✔ The upstairs master suite has a large walk-in closet and private bath.

✔ The secondary bedrooms share a hall bath.

Plan number ADA-1888-AJ91. See index for pricing details. Plan by Danielian Associates.

The diagrams presented here constitute only floor plans and elevations. Purchasers are advised to consult their state and local building regulations and a state-certified architect prior to any construction related to these plans.

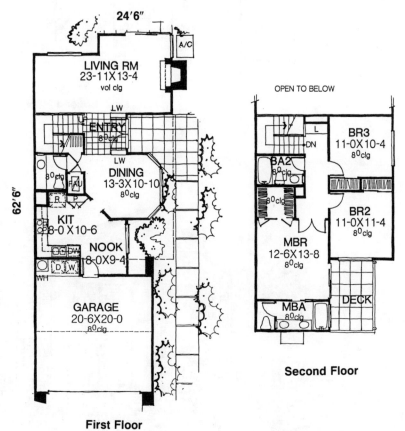

First Floor

Second Floor

Rear Elevation

Second Floor

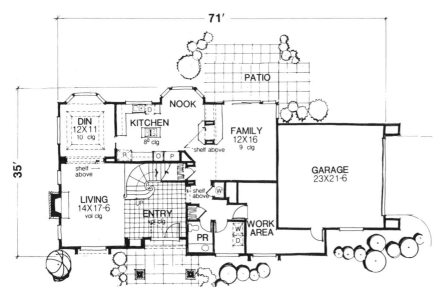

First Floor

Details Provide Two-Story Home With Strong Custom Appeal

First floor—1564 sq. ft.
Second floor—1365 sq. ft.
Total living space—2929 sq. ft.
4 bedrooms, 2½ baths
Shown with a concrete slab

✔ Spacious tile entry is graced by a gently curving staircase.

✔ Two-way fireplace adds drama to the family room and breakfast nook.

✔ The island in the kitchen adds counter space. The adjacent glass-enclosed breakfast bay floods the kitchen with natural light.

✔ Laundry room and mud room is conveniently located off the two-car garage.

Plan number ADA-1886-88MM. See index for pricing details. Plan by Danielian Associates.

The diagrams presented here constitute only floor plans and elevations. Purchasers are advised to consult their state and local building regulations and a state-certified architect prior to any construction related to these plans.

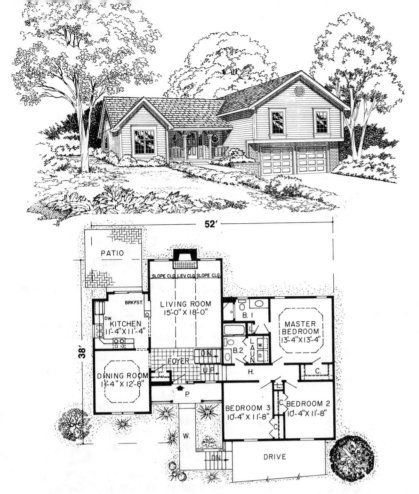

Split The Difference

Total living space—1459 sq. ft.
3 bedrooms, 2 baths
Shown with a basement

- Master bedroom has a private bath and a walk-in closet.

- Spacious kitchen has plenty of room for a table for informal meals.

- Bedrooms two and three share a hall bath.

- A 697-square-foot basement can be finished for additional living space.

- Laundry area is located in hall bath for convenience.

Plan number TGC-520-8611. See index for pricing details. Plan by The Garlinghouse Co.

The diagrams presented here constitute only floor plans and elevations. Purchasers are advised to consult their state and local building regulations and a state-certified architect prior to any construction related to these plans.

Skylights, Unique Ceiling Treatments Add To Design

Total living space—1774 sq. ft.
Unfinished bonus space—1399 sq. ft.
3 bedrooms, 2 baths
Shown with a basement

- The living room features a fireplace, wet bar, two skylights and a sloped ceiling.

- The kitchen features an eating island. The octagonal breakfast room features a sloped ceiling and access to the rear deck.

- A half stair leads to the master suite. The suite includes a walk-in closet, separate shower and tub, double-bowled vanity, tray ceiling and a window seat.

Plan number TGC-592-HS91. See index for pricing details. Plan by The Garlinghouse Co.

The diagrams presented here constitute only floor plans and elevations. Purchasers are advised to consult their state and local building regulations and a state-certified architect prior to any construction related to these plans.

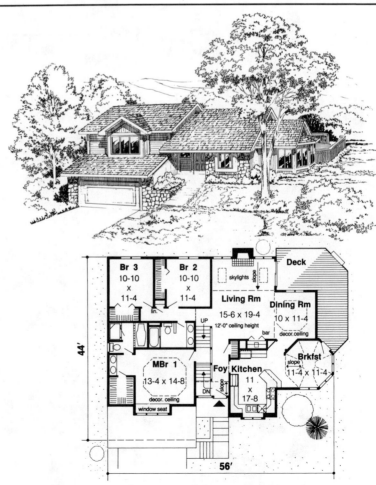

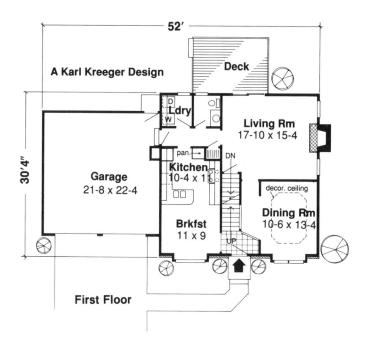

52'

A Karl Kreeger Design

30'4"

Deck

Ldry
D W

Living Rm
17-10 x 15-4

pan.

DN

Kitchen
10-4 x 13

decor. ceiling

Garage
21-8 x 22-4

Brkfst
11 x 9

Dining Rm
10-6 x 13-4

UP

First Floor

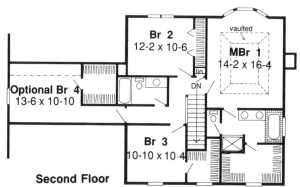

Br 2
12-2 x 10-6

vaulted

MBr 1
14-2 x 16-4

lin.

DN

Optional Br 4
13-6 x 10-10

Br 3
10-10 x 10-4

Second Floor

Living Room At Rear Of House Opens Onto A Deck

First floor—914 sq. ft.
Second floor—950 sq. ft.
Total living space—1864 sq. ft.
3 bedrooms, 2½ baths
Shown with a basement

- Living room at rear of house opens onto a deck

- Dining room features decor ceiling.

- Visual space expanded with kitchen opening into breakfast room.

- Highlights in master bedroom include vaulted ceiling and bay window.

- Optional fourth bedroom located over garage.

Plan number TGC-590-AJ92. See index for pricing details. Plan by The Garlinghouse Co.

The diagrams presented here constitute only floor plans and elevations. Purchasers are advised to consult their state and local building regulations and a state-certified architect prior to any construction related to these plans.

Combined Space Expands Interior

First floor—576 sq. ft.
Second floor—576 sq. ft.
Total living space—1152 sq. ft.
3 bedrooms, 1½ baths
Shown with a crawlspace

✔ Separate entry includes a coat closet, powder room access.

✔ Kitchen is designed to function efficiently.

✔ In-line arrangement of the living, dining rooms allow them to share views.

✔ Laundry facilities are located in the second-floor bath.

✔ Plan comes with an optional basement.

Plan number TNG-394-SU93. See index for pricing details. Plan by The Norris Group Inc.

The diagrams presented here constitute only floor plans and elevations. Purchasers are advised to consult their state and local building regulations and a state-certified architect prior to any construction related to these plans.

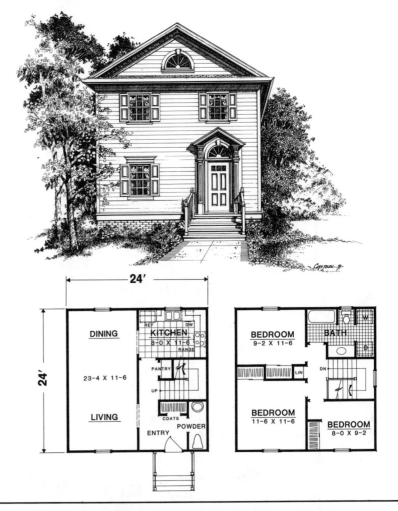

Covered Porch Expands Dining Space To The Outdoors

Total living space—2229 sq. ft.
3 bedrooms, 2 baths
Shown with a concrete slab

✔ Lovely display niche allows you to personalize the foyer with a valued treasure.

✔ Bookshelves, cabinets flank the fireplace in the living room.

✔ Wooden louver doors close the dining room off from the living area.

✔ French doors provide outdoor access to the covered porch and patio.

✔ Bay window provides breakfast area with an extra bright interior, outdoor views.

Plan number LWG-1006-9005. Plan by Larry W. Garnett & Associates Inc.

The diagrams presented here constitute only floor plans and elevations. Purchasers are advised to consult their state and local building regulations and a state-certified architect prior to any construction related to these plans.

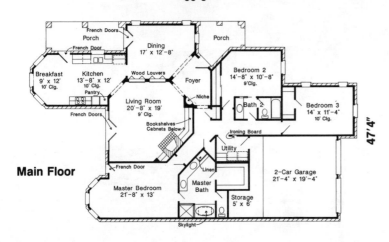

Main Floor

First Floor

NOOK 10/8 X 11/4 [9' CLG.]

FAMILY 14/4 X 21/0

DINING 11/8 X 13/8 [9' CLG.]

1 1/2 STORY **LIVING** 15/4 X 17/4

PLANTER

REF. PAN.

D. W.

DN.

UP

BUILT-IN

GARAGE 28/4 X 21/8

DEN 11/4 X 15/8

52'

57'

Second Floor

SPA

BR. 2 12/0 X 14/4

SKYLITE

MASTER 12/6 X 20/2 +/- [10'-8" CLG.]

BR. 3 10/4 X 12/0

LIVING RM. BELOW

DN.

LINEN

BR. 4 12/0 X 12/8

FOYER BELOW

ATTIC STORAGE

Suite Pleasure
For Masters Of This
Four-Bedroom Two Story

First floor—1643 sq. ft.
Second floor—1331 sq. ft.
Total living space—2974 sq. ft.
4 bedrooms, 2½ baths
Shown with a crawlspace

✔ Plan is designed for lots that slope to the rear as well as to the side.

✔ French doors hide the den which features a closet and built-in bookshelves.

✔ Living and family rooms have fireplaces.

✔ Open arrangement of the kitchen, family room and breakfast nook create a large informal zone.

✔ Attractive planter borders the formal dining area.

Plan number AMA-2488-SU93. See index for price details. Plan by Alan Mascord Design Associates.

The diagrams presented here constitute only floor plans and elevations. Purchasers are advised to consult their state and local building regulations and a state-certified architect prior to any construction related to these plans.

PLAN INDEX

Plan number	Paper	Price	Page
Barton & Associates Inc.			
TCB-1293-SU93	vellum	$306.00	34
TCB-1291-SU93	vellum	$300.00	35
TCB-1299-SU93	vellum	$435.00	34-35
TCB-1294-SU93	vellum	$341.40	46
TCB-1296-SU93	vellum	$300.00	46-47
TCB-1295-SU93	vellum	$300.00	47
Custom Creations Inc.			
CCI-2606-91M5	vellum	$300.00	19
CCI-2628-9207	vellum	$300.00	24
CCI-2692-AJ92	vellum	$300.00	42
CCI-2512-9010	vellum	$300.00	43
CCI-M2609-9107	vellum	$300.00	58
CCI-M2608-9107	vellum	$305.40	59
Danielian Associates			
ADA-1888-AJ91	vellum	$300.00	74
ADA-1886-88MM	vellum	$439.35	75
Design Traditions			
DTA-L2610-DT91	mylar	$434.70	2
DTA-2599-SU93	mylar	$332.25	29
DTA-M2609-DT91	mylar	$405.00	50
DTA-L2612-DT91	mylar	$429.75	51
DTA-L2619-DT91	mylar	$503.25	60
DTA-2597-AJ92	mylar	$300.00	61
Fillmore Design Group			
RFF-2112-8903	vellum	$300.00	54
Historical Replications Inc.			
HR-623-9207	mylar	$300.00	3
HR-689-88MM	mylar	$300.00	56
HR-601-8808	mylar	$300.00	57
HR-601-9104	mylar	$300.00	68
Homes For The Living			
HFL-M2704-9111	vellum	$326.85	69
HFL-2705-9202	vellum	$300.00	72
HFL-2701-9107	vellum	$300.00	73
The Norris Group			
TNG-M391-89MM	mylar	$372.00	25
TNG-396-SU93	mylar	$300.00	39
TNG-394-SU93	mylar	$300.00	78
Larry W. Garnett & Associates Inc.			
LWG-1091-SU93	mylar	$300.00	6
LWG-1090-SU93	mylar	$300.00	6
LWG-1089-SU93	mylar	$396.30	7
LWG-1088-SU93	mylar	$347.55	7
LWG-1002-91ZZ	mylar	$300.00	17
LWG-1008-91ZZ	mylar	$300.00	18
LWG-1010-87ZZ	mylar	$300.00	55
LWG-1099-SU93	mylar	$310.65	65
LWG-1006-9005	mylar	$334.35	78
Ralph Jones & Associates			
RJA-M2202-8905	vellum	$405.30	9
RJA-2201-91ZZ	vellum	$300.00	22-23
RJA-2207-9108	vellum	$300.00	24
RJA-2207-91ZZ	vellum	$518.55	30
RJA-M2231-90MN	vellum	$389.25	31
RJA-2205-91ZZ	vellum	$300.00	32
RJA-2203-91ZZ	vellum	$715.20	33
RJA-2200-91ZZ	vellum	$300.00	64
Design Profile Inc.			
DPI-M2302-8906	mylar	$368.70	10
DPI-2381-AJ92	mylar	$358.35	73
DPI-2399-SU93	mylar	$300.00	28
The Drees Company			
TDC-122A-92DC	mylar	$336.15	14-15
TDC-122B-92DC	mylar	$334.20	14-15
TDC-122C-92DC	mylar	$334.20	14-15
TDC-122D-92DC	mylar	$336.00	14-15
TDC-106A-92DC	mylar	$300.00	36
TDC-106B-92DC	mylar	$300.00	36
TDC-106C-92DC	mylar	$300.00	36
TDC-108A-92DC	mylar	$307.05	37
TDC-108B-92DC	mylar	$304.50	37
TDC-108C-92DC	mylar	$307.05	37
EDI Architecture/Planning			
EDI-1490-SU93	vellum	$318.00	11
EDI-1489-89MM	vellum	$312.60	16
Orchard House			
ORC-2997-AJ92	mylar	$300.00	12
ORC-2991-AJ92	mylar	$406.80	13
The Garlinghouse Co.			
TGC-595-SU93	vellum	$300.00	3
TGC-503-9104	vellum	$300.00	20
TGC-M593-HS91	vellum	$300.00	52
TGC-599-HS91	vellum	$300.00	53
TGC-520-8611	vellum	$300.00	76
TGC-592-HS91	vellum	$300.00	76
TGC-590-AJ92	vellum	$300.00	77
Quincy Johnson & Associates			
QJA-1991-SU93	mylar	$357.75	4
QJA-1989-SU93	mylar	$345.60	5
QJA-1911-8907	mylar	$300.00	8
QJA-1986-AJ92	mylar	$300.00	21
QJA-1998-AJ92	mylar	$300.00	26
QJA-1997-AJ92	mylar	$300.00	26
QJA-M1901-8805	mylar	$300.00	27
QJA-1995-AJ92	mylar	$300.00	70
QJA-1996-AJ92	mylar	$300.00	70
Kaufman & Meeks Inc.			
KM-796-9001	vellum	$300.00	48
KM-706-85MM	vellum	$300.00	49
KM-707-90MJ	vellum	$313.80	66
KM-708-90MJ	vellum	$313.80	66
KM-709-90MJ	vellum	$313.80	66
KM-702-85MM	vellum	$300.00	67
KM-798-86MM	vellum	$300.00	71
Alan Mascord Design Associates			
AMA-2402-DF93	mylar	$421.95	1
AMA-2498-SU93	mylar	$300.00	22
AMA-L2414-9110	mylar	$480.60	23
AMA-M2495-HS91	mylar	$329.70	38
AMA-L2486-HS91	mylar	$521.25	40
AMA-M2411-8907	mylar	$312.00	41
AMA-M2486-AJ91	mylar	$404.55	44
AMA-2417-89MO	mylar	$433.50	45
AMA-M2491-HS91	mylar	$408.00	62
AMA-2496-HS91	mylar	$589.35	63
AMA-2488-SU93	mylar	$446.10	79

ORDER FORM

Plans are available in standard blueline prints, mylar sepia or vellum prints. Prices are valid until December 31, 1993. *Professional Builder & Remodeler* will continue to accept orders from this magazine after that date, but prices are subject to change.

To charge on AMERICAN EXPRESS, MASTERCARD or VISA, call Toll Free 1-800-323-7379 (outside the United States call 708-635-8800) or send payment to:

Professional Builder & Remodeler
1350 E. Touhy Avenue,
P.O. Box 5080
Des Plaines, IL 60017-5080

☐ Check   ☐ Bill AMERICAN EXPRESS   ☐ Bill MASTERCARD   ☐ Bill VISA

I understand I will receive either 5 sets of bluelines, or a reproducible mylar or vellum. (Please refer to plan index to see which is available, mylar or vellum.) I would like to order the following plan numbers (homes under 2000 sq. ft. are a flat fee of $300.00).

_____   _____ × $0.15 = $_____
Plan Number   Total sq. ft.
☐ 5 bluelines   ☐ mylars   ☐ vellums

_____   _____ × $0.15 = $_____
Plan Number   Total sq. ft.
☐ 5 bluelines   ☐ mylars   ☐ vellums

_____   _____ × $0.15 = $_____
Plan Number   Total sq. ft.
☐ 5 bluelines   ☐ mylars   ☐ vellums

How do you wish to receive your house plans?
☐ U.S. mail ($8.00)   = $_____
☐ Express mail—2-3 working days ($20.00)   = $_____
☐ Overnight mail ($50.00)   = $_____
☐ Canada express mail ($30.00)   = $_____
☐ Canada overnight mail ($60.00)   = $_____
NOTE: These charges are per each architect

Handling charges payable on all orders   = $ 5.00

Total of order $_____

Send order to:

Name_____

Company name_____

Address_____
(cannot be delivered to a Post Office Box)

City/State/Zip Code_____

Daytime phone with area code_____

Credit card number_____

Expiration date_____

Use Our Toll-Free Number:
1-800-323-7379

Plans are nonreturnable

BNi Building News™
Costbook

BNi Building News™
Los Angeles • Boston

Preface

For the past 47 years, *Building News* has been dedicated to providing construction professionals with timely and reliable information. Based on this experience, our staff has researched and compiled thousands of up-to-the minute costs for the second annual editions of *Building News Costbooks.*

This book is an essential reference for contractors, engineers, architects, facilities managers-any construction professional who must provide an estimate on any type of building project.

Whether working up a preliminary estimate or submitting a formal bid, the costs listed here can quickly and easily be tailored to your needs. All costs are based on national averages, while a table of modifiers is provided for regional adjustments. Overhead and profit are included in all costs.

All data is categorized according to the MASTER-FORMAT of the Construction Specifications Institute (CSI). This industry standard provides an all-inclusive checklist to ensure that no element of a project is overlooked. In addition, to make specific items even easier to locate, there is a complete alphabetical index.

The "Features in this Book" section presents a clear overview of the many features of this book. Included is an explanation of the data, sample page layout and discussion of how to best use the information in the book.

Of course, all buildings and construction projects are unique. The costs provided in this book are based on averages from well-managed projects with good labor productivity under normal working conditions (eight hours a day). Other circumstances affecting costs such as overtime, unusual or hidden costs must be factored in as they arise.

The data provided in this book is for estimating purposes only. Check all applicable federal, state and local codes and regulations for specific requirements.

Editor-In-Chief
William D. Mahoney

Contributing Editors
Kenneth M. Randall
Edward B. Wetherill

Technical Services
Anthony Jackson
Ramon Lopez
Rita Wong

Design
Robert O. Wright

BNI Publications, Inc.

3055 Overland Avenue
Los Angeles, CA 90034
(310) 202-7775

77 Wexford Street
Needham Heights, MA 02194
(617) 455-1466

Geographic Cost Modifiers

The costs as presented in this book attempt to represent national averages. Costs, however, vary among regions, states and even between adjacent localities.

In order to more closely approximate the probable costs for specific locations throughout the U.S., this table of Geographic Cost Modifiers is provided. These adjustment factors are used to modify costs obtained from this book to help account for regional variations of construction costs and to provide a more accurate estimate for specific areas. The factors are formulated by comparing costs in a specific area to the costs as presented in the Costbook pages. An example of how to use these factors is shown below. Whenever local current costs are known, whether material prices or labor rates, they should be used when more accuracy is required.

$$\begin{array}{ccc} \text{Cost obtained} & \text{Location Cost} & \\ \text{from Costbook} \times & \text{Adjustment} = & \text{Adjusted Cost} \\ \text{pages} & \text{Factor} & \end{array}$$

For example, a project estimated to cost $125,000 using the Costbook pages can be adjusted to more closely approximate the cost in Los Angeles: $125,000 × 1.07 = $133,750.

Alabama	0.78
Alaska	1.35
Arizona	0.88
Arkansas	0.72
California	
Los Angeles	1.07
San Francisco	1.21
Other	1.01
Colorado	0.87
Connecticut	1.02
Delaware	0.90
Florida	0.80
Georgia	
Atlanta	0.81
Other	0.73
Hawaii	1.20
Idaho	0.86
Illinois	
Chicago	0.99
Other	0.93
Indiana	0.88
Iowa	0.86
Kansas	0.80
Kentucky	0.83
Louisiana	0.84
Maine	0.87
Maryland	0.89
Massachusetts	
Boston	1.05
Other	0.98
Michigan	0.90
Minnesota	0.91
Missouri	0.84
Montana	0.85
Nebraska	0.81
Nevada	0.93
New Hampshire	0.88
New Jersey	0.98
New Mexico	0.82
New York	
New York City	1.24
Other	0.93
North Carolina	0.73
North Dakota	0.85
Ohio	0.86
Oklahoma	0.77
Oregon	0.89
Pennsylvania	
Philadelphia	1.03
Other	0.89
Rhode Island	0.99
South Carolina	0.75
South Dakota	0.75
Tennessee	0.78
Texas	0.80
Utah	0.81
Vermont	0.86
Virginia	0.81
Washington	1.00
Washington D.C.	0.93
West Virginia	0.86
Wisconsin	0.91
Wyoming	0.86

Features In This Book

Sample pages with graphic explanations are included before the Costbook pages and Man-Hour Tables. These explanations along with the discussions below, will provide a good understanding of what is included in this book and how it can best be used in construction estimating.

Material Costs

The material costs used in this book represent national averages for prices that a contractor would expect to pay plus an allowance for freight (if applicable), handling and storage. These costs reflect neither the lowest or highest prices, but rather a typical average cost over time. Periodic fluctuations in availability and in certain commodities (eg. cooper, lumber) can significantly affect local material pricing. In the final estimating and bidding stages of a project when the highest degree of accuracy is required, it is best to check local, current prices.

Labor Costs

Labor costs include the basic wage, plus commonly applicable taxes, insurance and markups for overhead and profit. The labor rates used here to develop the costs are typical average prevailing wage rates. Rates for different trades are used where appropriate for each type of work.

Taxes and insurance which are most often applied to labor rates included employer-paid Social Security/Medicare taxes (FICA), Worker's Compensation insurance, state and federal unemployment taxes, and business insurance. Fixed government rates as well as average allowances are included in the labor costs. However, most of these items vary significantly from state to state and within states. For more specific data, local agencies and sources should be consulted.

Equipment Costs

Cost for various types and pieces of equipment are included in Division I—General Requirements and can be included in an estimate when required either as a total "Equipment" category or with specific appropriate trades. Costs for equipment are included when appropriate in the installation of costs in the Costbook pages.

Overhead And Profit

Included in the labor costs are allowances for overhead and profit for the contractor/employer whose workers are performing the specific tasks. No cost allowances or fees are included for man-agement of subcontractors by the general contractor or construction manager. These cost, where appropriate, must be added to the costs as listed in the book.

The allowance for overhead is included to account for office overhead, the contractors' typical costs of doing business. These costs normally include in-house office staff salaries and benefits, office rent and operating expenses, professional fees, vehicle costs and other operating costs which are not directly applicable to specific jobs. It should be noted for this book that office overhead as included should be distinguished from project overhead, the General Requirements (CSI Division 1) which are specific to particular projects. Project overhead should be included on an item by item basis for each job.

Depending on the trade, an allowance of 10 to 15 percent is incorporated into the labor/installation costs to account for typical profit of the installing contractor. See Division 1, General Requirements, for a more detailed review of typical profit allowances.

Adjustments to Costs

The costs as presented in this book attempt to represent national averages. Costs, however, vary among regions, states and even between adjacent localities.

In order to more closely approximate the probable costs for specific locations throughout the U.S., a table of Geographic Cost Modifiers is provided. These adjustment factors are used to modify costs obtained from this book to help account for regional variations of construction costs. Whenever local current cost are known, whether material or equipment prices or labor rates, they should be used if more accuracy is required.

Editors' Note: *The Building News Costbooks* are intended to provide accurate, reliable, average costs and typical productivities for thousands of common construction components. The data is developed and compiled from various industry sources, including government, manufacturers, suppliers and working professionals. The intent of the information is to provide assistance and guidelines to construction professionals in estimating. The user should be aware that local conditions, material and labor availability and cost variations, economic considerations, weather, local codes and regulations, etc., all affect the actual cost of construction. These and other such factors must be considered and incorporated into any and all construction estimates.

Sample Costbook Page

In order to best use the information in this book, please review this sample page and read the "Features In This Book" section.

CSI MASTERFORMAT Division

CSI Broadscope Category

CSI Mediumscope Category (First 5 Digits)

Detailed Descriptions

Complete descriptions of items may include information listed above a particular line. Review of the whole category is recommended for a complete description.

Material Cost

Material costs represent average contractor prices plus an allowance for freight, handling and storage.

Installation Cost

Installation costs include basic wage rates, markups for taxes, insurance overhead and profit and also include equipment costs where appropriate.

Total Cost

The total cost is the sum of material and installation costs. This total represents typical contractors' costs including overhead and profit, but does not include markups for the general contractor or construction management fees.

Unit of Measurement

Each item (and cost) is defined in terms of the common estimating unit. All costs are listed in dollars per unit.

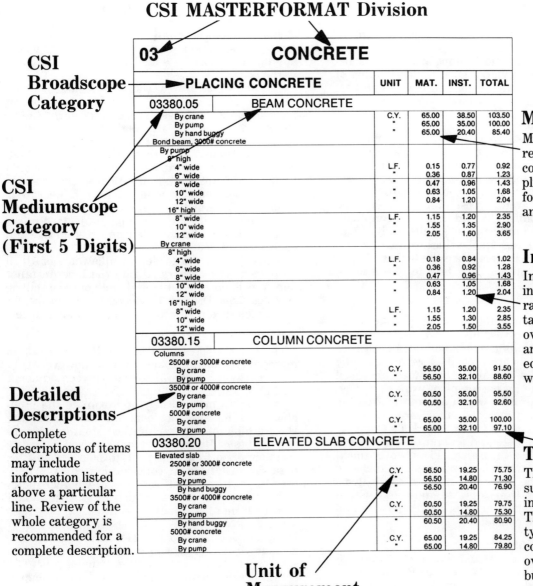

03	CONCRETE				
PLACING CONCRETE		UNIT	MAT.	INST.	TOTAL
03380.05	BEAM CONCRETE				
By crane		C.Y.	65.00	38.50	103.50
By pump		"	65.00	35.00	100.00
By hand buggy		"	65.00	20.40	85.40
Bond beam, 3000# concrete					
By pump					
8" high					
4" wide		L.F.	0.15	0.77	0.92
6" wide		"	0.36	0.87	1.23
8" wide		"	0.47	0.96	1.43
10" wide		"	0.63	1.05	1.68
12" wide		"	0.84	1.20	2.04
16" high					
8" wide		L.F.	1.15	1.20	2.35
10" wide		"	1.55	1.35	2.90
12" wide		"	2.05	1.60	3.65
By crane					
8" high					
4" wide		L.F.	0.18	0.84	1.02
6" wide		"	0.36	0.92	1.28
8" wide		"	0.47	0.96	1.43
10" wide		"	0.63	1.05	1.68
12" wide		"	0.84	1.20	2.04
16" high					
8" wide		L.F.	1.15	1.20	2.35
10" wide		"	1.55	1.30	2.85
12" wide		"	2.05	1.50	3.55
03380.15	COLUMN CONCRETE				
Columns					
2500# or 3000# concrete					
By crane		C.Y.	56.50	35.00	91.50
By pump		"	56.50	32.10	88.60
3500# or 4000# concrete					
By crane		C.Y.	60.50	35.00	95.50
By pump		"	60.50	32.10	92.60
5000# concrete					
By crane		C.Y.	65.00	35.00	100.00
By pump		"	65.00	32.10	97.10
03380.20	ELEVATED SLAB CONCRETE				
Elevated slab					
2500# or 3000# concrete					
By crane		C.Y.	56.50	19.25	75.75
By pump		"	56.50	14.80	71.30
By hand buggy		"	56.50	20.40	76.90
3500# or 4000# concrete					
By crane		C.Y.	60.50	19.25	79.75
By pump		"	60.50	14.80	75.30
By hand buggy		"	60.50	20.40	80.90
5000# concrete					
By crane		C.Y.	65.00	19.25	84.25
By pump		"	65.00	14.80	79.80

REQUIREMENTS	UNIT	MAT.	INST.	TOTAL
01500.10 TEMPORARY FACILITIES				
Trailers, general office type, per month				
Minimum	EA.			110.00
Average	"			220.00
Maximum	"			440.00
01525.10 CONSTRUCTION AIDS				
Scaffolding/staging, rent per month				
Measured by lineal feet of base				
10' high	L.F.			6.60
20' high	"			11.00
01600.10 EQUIPMENT				
Air compressor				
60 cfm				
By day	EA.			55.00
By week	"			165.00
By month	"			495.00
Generators, 5 kw				
By day	EA.			44.00
By week	"			132.00
By month	"			396.00
Heaters, salamander type, per week				
Minimum	EA.			55.00
Average	"			82.50
Maximum	"			110.00
Pumps, submersible				
50 gpm				
By day	EA.			44.00
By week	"			132.00
By month	"			396.00
Pickup truck				
By day	EA.			110.00
By week	"			330.00
By month	"			990.00
Dump truck				
6 cy truck				
By day	EA.			220.00
By week	"			660.00
By month	"			1,980
16 cy truck				
By day	EA.			275.00
By week	"			825.00
By month	"			2,420
Backhoe, track mounted				
1 cy capacity				
By day	EA.			660.00
By week	"			1,980
By month	"			5,940
3 cy capacity				
By day	EA.			1,650
By week	"			4,950
By month	"			14,850

REQUIREMENTS	UNIT	MAT.	INST.	TOTAL
01600.10 EQUIPMENT				
Bulldozer				
75 hp				
By day	EA.			440.00
By week	"			1,320
By month	"			3,960
200 hp				
By day	EA.			880.00
By week	"			2,640
By month	"			7,920
Cranes, crawler type				
15 ton capacity				
By day	EA.			440.00
By week	"			1,320
By month	"			3,960
Truck mounted, hydraulic				
15 ton capacity				
By day	EA.			440.00
By week	"			1,320
By month	"			3,960
Loader, rubber tired				
1 cy capacity				
By day	EA.			440.00
By week	"			1,320
By month	"			3,960
2 cy capacity				
By day	EA.			550.00
By week	"			1,650
By month	"			4,950
01740.10 BONDS				
Performance bonds				
Minimum	PCT			1.00
Average	"			2.00
Maximum	"			3.00

DEMOLITION	UNIT	MAT.	INST.	TOTAL
02060.10 BUILDING DEMOLITION				
Building, complete with disposal				
Wood frame	C.F.	0.00	0.15	0.15
Concrete	"	0.00	0.23	0.23
Steel frame	"	0.00	0.30	0.30
Partition removal				
Brick masonry partitions				
8" thick	S.F.	0.00	1.25	1.25
Stud partitions				
Metal or wood, with drywall both sides	S.F.	0.00	1.00	1.00
Door and frame removal				
Single				
2'6"x6'8"	EA.	0.00	14.55	14.55
3'x6'8"	"	0.00	17.00	17.00
Double				
2'6"x6'8"	EA.	0.00	20.40	20.40
3'x6'8"	"	0.00	22.65	22.65
Floor removal				
Residential wood	S.F.	0.00	0.58	0.58
Resilient tile or linoleum	"	0.00	0.20	0.20
Ceiling removal				
Acoustical tile ceiling				
Adhesive fastened	S.F.	0.00	0.20	0.20
Suspended grid	"	0.00	0.13	0.13
Drywall ceiling				
Nailed to framing	S.F.	0.00	0.20	0.20
Plastered ceiling				
Furred on framing	S.F.	0.00	0.51	0.51
Roofing removal				
Built up roof on wood deck	S.F.	0.00	0.63	0.63
Roof shingles	"	0.00	0.34	0.34
Window removal				
Metal windows, trim included				
2'x3'	EA.	0.00	20.40	20.40
3'x4'	"	0.00	25.50	25.50
Wood windows, trim included				
2'x3'	EA.	0.00	20.40	20.40
3'x4'	"	0.00	13.60	13.60
02065.15 SAW CUTTING PAVEMENT				
Pavement, bituminous				
2" thick	L.F.	0.00	0.80	0.80
3" thick	"	0.00	1.00	1.00
Concrete pavement, with wire mesh				
4" thick	L.F.	0.00	1.55	1.55
6" thick	"	0.00	1.80	1.80
02080.15 PIPE INSULATION REMOVAL				
Removal, asbestos insulation				
2" thick, pipe				
1" to 3" dia.	L.F.	0.00	1.70	1.70
4" to 6" dia.	"	0.00	1.95	1.95

DEMOLITION	UNIT	MAT.	INST.	TOTAL
02080.15 PIPE INSULATION REMOVAL				
3" thick				
7" to 8" dia.	L.F.	0.00	2.05	2.05
15" to 18" dia.	"	0.00	2.55	2.55

SITE DEMOLITION	UNIT	MAT.	INST.	TOTAL
02105.20 FENCES				
Remove fencing				
Chain link, 8' high				
For disposal	L.F.	0.00	1.00	1.00
For reuse	"	0.00	2.55	2.55
Wood				
4' high	EA.	0.00	0.68	0.68
6' high	"	0.00	0.82	0.82
Masonry				
8" thick				
4' high	EA.	0.00	2.05	2.05
6' high	"	0.00	2.55	2.55
8' high	"	0.00	2.90	2.90
02105.42 DRAINAGE PIPING				
Remove drainage pipe, not including excavation				
12" dia.	L.F.	0.00	4.60	4.60
18" dia.	"	0.00	5.80	5.80
02105.43 GAS PIPING				
Remove welded steel pipe, not including excavation				
4" dia.	L.F.	0.00	6.85	6.85
6" dia.	"	0.00	13.75	13.75
02105.45 SANITARY PIPING				
Remove sewer pipe, not including excavation				
4" dia.	L.F.	0.00	4.40	4.40
8" dia.	"	0.00	5.50	5.50
02105.48 WATER PIPING				
Remove water pipe, not including excavation				
4" dia.	L.F.	0.00	5.50	5.50
8" dia.	"	0.00	6.10	6.10

02 SITEWORK

SITE DEMOLITION	UNIT	MAT.	INST.	TOTAL
02105.60 UNDERGROUND TANKS				
Remove underground storage tank, and backfill 1000 gals	EA.	0.00	275.00	275.00
02105.66 SEPTIC TANKS				
Remove septic tank 1000 gals	EA.	0.00	91.50	91.50
02105.80 WALLS, EXTERIOR				
Concrete wall Medium reinforcing 6" thick	S.F.	0.00	8.45	8.45
8" thick	"	0.00	9.15	9.15
Masonry 8" thick	S.F.	0.00	3.15	3.15
12" thick	"	0.00	3.65	3.65
02110.50 TREE CUTTING & CLEARING				
Cut trees and clear out stumps 9" to 12" dia.	EA.	0.00	220.00	220.00
To 24" dia.	"	0.00	275.00	275.00

EARTHWORK	UNIT	MAT.	INST.	TOTAL
02210.10 HAULING MATERIAL				
Haul material by 10 cy dump truck, round trip distance 5 mile	C.Y.	0.00	3.35	3.35
Site grading, cut & fill, sandy clay, 200' haul, 75 hp dozer	"	0.00	1.60	1.60
Spread topsoil by equipment on site	"	0.00	1.80	1.80
Site grading (cut and fill to 6") less than 1 acre 75 hp dozer	C.Y.	0.00	2.65	2.65
1.5 cy backhoe/loader	"	0.00	4.00	4.00
02210.30 BULK EXCAVATION				
Hydraulic excavator Medium material	C.Y.	0.00	2.20	2.20
Wheel mounted front-end loader Medium material	C.Y.	0.00	1.60	1.60
Track mounted front-end loader Medium material	C.Y.	0.00	1.00	1.00

/5

EARTHWORK	UNIT	MAT.	INST.	TOTAL
02220.40 BUILDING EXCAVATION				
Structural excavation, unclassified earth				
3/8 cy backhoe	C.Y.	0.00	7.40	7.40
1 cy backhoe	"	0.00	4.65	4.65
Foundation backfill and compaction by machine	"	0.00	11.10	11.10
02220.60 TRENCHING				
Trenching and continuous footing excavation				
By gradall				
Medium soil	C.Y.	0.00	1.70	1.70
By hydraulic excavator				
Medium soil	C.Y.	0.00	2.00	2.00
Hand excavation				
Normal soil	C.Y.	0.00	22.65	22.65
Sand or gravel	"	0.00	25.50	25.50
Backfill trenches				
With compaction				
By hand	C.Y.	0.00	17.00	17.00
By 60 hp tracked dozer	"	0.00	1.00	1.00
02220.90 HAND EXCAVATION				
Excavation				
To 2' deep				
Normal soil	C.Y.	0.00	22.65	22.65
To 6' deep				
Normal soil	C.Y.	0.00	29.10	29.10
Excavation around obstructions and services	"	0.00	68.00	68.00
02270.40 RIPRAP				
Riprap				
Stone quarry run, max size 300 lb. stones	TON	22.00	27.90	49.90
400 lb. stones	"	22.00	25.90	47.90
750 lb. stones	"	22.00	22.70	44.70
02280.20 SOIL TREATMENT				
Soil treatment, termite control pretreatment, under slabs	S.F.	0.07	0.11	0.18
By walls	"	0.07	0.14	0.21

PAVING AND SURFACING	UNIT	MAT.	INST.	TOTAL
02510.20 ASPHALT SURFACES				
Asphalt wearing surface, for flexible pavement				
1" thick	S.Y.	1.65	1.00	2.65
1-1/2" thick	"	2.50	1.20	3.70
Bituminous sidewalk, no base				

02   SITEWORK

PAVING AND SURFACING	UNIT	MAT.	INST.	TOTAL
02510.20 ASPHALT SURFACES				
2" thick	S.Y.	3.60	1.30	4.90
02520.10 CONCRETE PAVING				
Concrete paving, reinforced, 5000 psi concrete				
6" thick	S.Y.	14.45	9.55	24.00
8" thick	"	18.25	10.90	29.15
10" thick	"	21.95	12.70	34.65
02810.40 LAWN IRRIGATION				
Residential system, complete				
Minimum	ACRE			11,000
Maximum	"			16,500
02830.10 CHAIN LINK FENCE				
Chain link fence, 9 ga., galvanized, with posts 10' o.c.				
4' high	L.F.	3.85	1.45	5.30
6' high	"	5.80	2.55	8.35
Swing gates, galvanized, 4' high				
Single gate				
3' wide	EA.	116.00	51.00	167.00
4' wide	"	126.00	51.00	177.00
Double gate				
10' wide	EA.	297.00	81.50	378.50

FORMWORK	UNIT	MAT.	INST.	TOTAL
03110.05 BEAM FORMWORK				
Beam forms, job built				
Beam bottoms				
1 use	S.F.	2.65	4.30	6.95
5 uses	"	0.86	3.65	4.51
Beam sides				
1 use	S.F.	1.85	2.85	4.70
5 uses	"	0.75	2.35	3.10
03110.15 COLUMN FORMWORK				
Column, square forms, job built				
8" x 8" columns				
1 use	S.F.	2.20	5.15	7.35
5 uses	"	0.77	4.45	5.22
12" x 12" columns				
1 use	S.F.	2.10	4.70	6.80
5 uses	"	0.66	4.10	4.76
03110.20 ELEVATED SLAB FORMWORK				
Elevated slab formwork				
1 use	S.F.	2.05	2.05	4.10
5 uses	"	0.74	1.75	2.49
03110.25 EQUIPMENT PAD FORMWORK				
Equipment pad, job built				
1 use	S.F.	2.10	3.20	5.30
3 uses	"	0.99	2.85	3.84
03110.35 FOOTING FORMWORK				
Wall footings, job built, continuous				
1 use	S.F.	0.80	2.55	3.35
5 uses	"	0.30	2.15	2.45
Column footings, spread				
1 use	S.F.	0.96	3.20	4.16
5 uses	"	0.30	2.55	2.85
03110.50 GRADE BEAM FORMWORK				
Grade beams, job built				
1 use	S.F.	1.65	2.55	4.20
5 uses	"	0.50	2.15	2.65
03110.55 SLAB/MAT FORMWORK				
Mat foundations, job built				
1 use	S.F.	1.55	3.20	4.75
5 uses	"	0.44	2.55	2.99

03 CONCRETE

FORMWORK		UNIT	MAT.	INST.	TOTAL
03110.65	**WALL FORMWORK**				
Wall forms, exterior, job built					
Up to 8' high wall					
1 use		S.F.	1.75	2.55	4.30
5 uses		"	0.63	2.15	2.78

REINFORCEMENT		UNIT	MAT.	INST.	TOTAL
03210.05	**BEAM REINFORCING**				
Beam-girders					
#3 - #4		TON	638.00	731.00	1,369
#5 - #6		"	578.00	585.00	1,163
03210.15	**COLUMN REINFORCING**				
Columns					
#3 - #4		TON	638.00	835.00	1,473
#5 - #6		"	578.00	650.00	1,228
03210.20	**ELEVATED SLAB REINFORCING**				
Elevated slab					
#3 - #4		TON	638.00	366.00	1,004
#5 - #6		"	578.00	325.00	903.00
03210.25	**EQUIP. PAD REINFORCING**				
Equipment pad					
#3 - #4		TON	638.00	585.00	1,223
#5 - #6		"	578.00	532.00	1,110
03210.35	**FOOTING REINFORCING**				
Footings					
#3 - #4		TON	638.00	487.00	1,125
#5 - #6		"	578.00	418.00	996.00
03210.45	**FOUNDATION REINFORCING**				
Foundations					
#3 - #4		TON	638.00	487.00	1,125
#5 - #6		"	578.00	418.00	996.00

03 CONCRETE

REINFORCEMENT		UNIT	MAT.	INST.	TOTAL
03210.50	GRADE BEAM REINFORCING				
Grade beams					
#3 - #4		TON	638.00	450.00	1,088
#5 - #6		"	578.00	390.00	968.00
03210.55	SLAB/MAT REINFORCING				
Bars, slabs					
#3 - #4		TON	638.00	487.00	1,125
#5 - #6		"	578.00	418.00	996.00
Wire mesh, slabs					
Galvanized					
4x4					
W1.4xW1.4		S.F.	0.22	0.19	0.41
W4.0xW4.0		"	0.57	0.24	0.81
6x6					
W1.4xW1.4		S.F.	0.15	0.15	0.30
W4.0xW4.0		"	0.42	0.19	0.61
03210.65	WALL REINFORCING				
Walls					
#3 - #4		TON	638.00	418.00	1,056
#5 - #6		"	578.00	366.00	944.00

CAST-IN-PLACE CONCRETE		UNIT	MAT.	INST.	TOTAL
03300.10	CONCRETE ADMIXTURES				
Concrete admixtures					
Water reducing admixture		GAL			9.35
Set retarder		"			16.50
Floor finishes					
Broom		S.F.	0.00	0.29	0.29
Float		"	0.00	0.34	0.34

03 CONCRETE

PLACING CONCRETE	UNIT	MAT.	INST.	TOTAL
03380.05 BEAM CONCRETE				
2500# or 3000# concrete				
By crane	C.Y.	56.50	38.50	95.00
By pump	"	56.50	35.00	91.50
By hand buggy	"	56.50	20.40	76.90
03380.15 COLUMN CONCRETE				
2500# or 3000# concrete				
By crane	C.Y.	56.50	35.00	91.50
By pump	"	56.50	32.10	88.60
03380.25 EQUIPMENT PAD CONCRETE				
Equipment pad				
2500# or 3000# concrete				
By chute	C.Y.	56.50	6.80	63.30
By pump	"	56.50	27.50	84.00
By crane	"	56.50	32.10	88.60
03380.35 FOOTING CONCRETE				
Continuous footing				
2500# or 3000# concrete				
By chute	C.Y.	56.50	6.80	63.30
By pump	"	56.50	24.05	80.55
By crane	"	56.50	27.50	84.00
Spread footing				
2500# or 3000# concrete				
By chute	C.Y.	56.50	6.80	63.30
By pump	"	56.50	25.70	82.20
By crane	"	56.50	29.60	86.10
03380.50 GRADE BEAM CONCRETE				
Grade beam				
2500# or 3000# concrete				
By chute	C.Y.	56.50	6.80	63.30
By crane	"	56.50	27.50	84.00
By pump	"	56.50	24.05	80.55
By hand buggy	"	56.50	20.40	76.90
03380.55 SLAB/MAT CONCRETE				
Slab on grade				
2500# or 3000# concrete				
By chute	C.Y.	56.50	5.10	61.60
By crane	"	56.50	16.05	72.55
By pump	"	56.50	13.75	70.25
By hand buggy	"	56.50	13.60	70.10
03380.58 SIDEWALKS				
Walks, cast in place with wire mesh, base not incl.				
4" thick	S.F.	0.78	0.68	1.46
5" thick	"	1.05	0.82	1.87

03 CONCRETE

PLACING CONCRETE	UNIT	MAT.	INST.	TOTAL
03380.58 SIDEWALKS				
6" thick	S.F.	1.25	1.00	2.25
03380.65 WALL CONCRETE				
Walls				
2500# or 3000#				
To 4'				
By chute	C.Y.	56.50	5.85	62.35
By crane	"	56.50	32.10	88.60
By pump	"	56.50	29.60	86.10
To 8'				
By crane	C.Y.	56.50	35.00	91.50
By pump	"	56.50	32.10	88.60
Filled block (CMU)				
3000# concrete, by pump				
4" wide	S.F.	0.21	1.35	1.56
6" wide	"	0.47	1.60	2.07
8" wide	"	0.74	1.90	2.64

04 MASONRY

MORTAR AND GROUT	UNIT	MAT.	INST.	TOTAL
04100.10 MASONRY GROUT				
Grout-filled concrete block (CMU)				
4" wide	S.F.	0.26	0.92	1.18
6" wide	"	0.56	1.00	1.56
8" wide	"	1.05	1.10	2.15
04150.10 MASONRY ACCESSORIES				
Rectangular wall ties				
3/16" dia., galvanized				
2" x 6"	EA.	0.13	0.42	0.55
2" x 8"	"	0.14	0.42	0.56
"Z" type wall ties, galvanized				
6" long				
1/8" dia.	EA.	0.13	0.42	0.55
8" long				
1/8" dia.	EA.	0.14	0.42	0.56
Brick anchors				
Corrugated, 3-1/2" long				
16 ga.	EA.	0.12	0.42	0.54

UNIT MASONRY	UNIT	MAT.	INST.	TOTAL
04210.10 BRICK MASONRY				
Standard size brick, running bond				
Face brick, red (6.4/sf)				
Veneer	S.F.	1.80	4.20	6.00
9" solid wall	"	3.95	7.20	11.15
Select common for veneers	"	2.00	4.20	6.20
04210.60 PAVERS, MASONRY				
Brick walk laid on sand, sand joints				
Laid flat, (4.5 per sf)	S.F.	1.10	2.80	3.90
Laid on edge, (7.2 per sf)	"	1.65	4.20	5.85
Precast concrete patio blocks				
Natural	S.F.	0.83	0.84	1.67
Colors	"	1.05	0.84	1.89
Bluestone				
Irregular	S.F.	1.55	6.30	7.85
Snapped rectangular	"	2.70	5.05	7.75
Slate				
Irregular, 3/4" thick	S.F.	1.45	7.20	8.65
Crushed stone, white marble, 3" thick	"	0.55	0.41	0.96

UNIT MASONRY	UNIT	MAT.	INST.	TOTAL
04220.10 CONCRETE MASONRY UNITS				
Hollow, load bearing				
4"	S.F.	1.05	1.85	2.90
8"	"	1.85	2.10	3.95
12"	"	2.60	2.50	5.10
Solid, load bearing				
4"	S.F.	1.55	1.85	3.40
8"	"	2.10	2.10	4.20
12"	"	3.05	2.50	5.55
Back-up block, sand aggregate, 8" x 16"				
2"	S.F.	0.76	1.45	2.21
4"	"	1.10	1.50	2.60
6"	"	1.35	1.55	2.90
8"	"	1.60	1.70	3.30

STONE	UNIT	MAT.	INST.	TOTAL
04400.10 STONE				
Rubble stone				
Walls set in mortar				
8" thick	S.F.	8.25	6.30	14.55
24" thick	"	16.50	16.75	33.25
Dry set wall				
8" thick	S.F.	9.35	4.20	13.55
24" thick	"	17.60	10.05	27.65
Cut stone				
Facing panels				
3/4" thick	S.F.	22.00	10.05	32.05
1-1/2" thick	"	33.00	11.45	44.45
04550.10 REFRACTORIES				
Flue liners				
Rectangular				
8" x 12"	L.F.	4.05	4.20	8.25
12" x 12"	"	5.50	4.55	10.05

METAL FASTENING	UNIT	MAT.	INST.	TOTAL
05050.10 STRUCTURAL WELDING				
Welding				
Single pass				
1/8"	L.F.	0.34	1.45	1.79
3/16"	"	0.68	1.90	2.58
1/4"	"	0.91	2.40	3.31
05050.90 METAL ANCHORS				
Anchor bolts				
3/8" x				
8" long	EA.			2.75
10" long	"			2.95
12" long	"			3.20
1/2" x				
8" long	EA.			3.85
10" long	"			3.95
12" long	"			4.30
Expansion shield				
1/4"	EA.			0.44
3/8"	"			0.72
1/2"	"			1.15
Non-drilling anchor				
1/4"	EA.			0.33
3/8"	"			0.45
1/2"	"			0.70
Self-drilling anchor				
1/4"	EA.			0.44
3/8"	"			0.68
1/2"	"			1.00

COLD FORMED FRAMING	UNIT	MAT.	INST.	TOTAL
05410.10 METAL FRAMING				
Furring channel, galvanized				
Beams and columns, 3/4"				
12" o.c.	S.F.	0.33	2.85	3.18
16" o.c.	"	0.28	2.60	2.88
Walls, 3/4"				
12" o.c.	S.F.	0.33	1.45	1.78
16" o.c.	"	0.28	1.20	1.48
24" o.c.	"	0.22	0.95	1.17
Stud, load bearing				
16" o.c.				

COLD FORMED FRAMING	UNIT	MAT.	INST.	TOTAL
05410.10 METAL FRAMING				
16 ga.				
2-1/2"	S.F.	0.92	1.25	2.17
3-5/8"	"	1.10	1.25	2.35
4"	"	1.15	1.25	2.40
24" o.c.				
16 ga.				
2-1/2"	S.F.	0.55	1.10	1.65
3-5/8"	"	0.64	1.10	1.74
4"	"	0.75	1.10	1.85
6"	"	0.89	1.20	2.09
05520.10 RAILINGS				
Railing, pipe				
1-1/4" diameter, welded steel				
2-rail				
Primed	L.F.	14.85	5.70	20.55
Galvanized	"	17.85	5.70	23.55
3-rail				
Primed	L.F.	19.50	7.15	26.65
Galvanized	"	23.55	7.15	30.70
1-1/2" diameter, welded steel				
2-rail				
Primed	L.F.	18.10	5.70	23.80
Galvanized	"	21.70	5.70	27.40
3-rail				
Primed	L.F.	23.75	7.15	30.90
Galvanized	"	28.50	7.15	35.65
05700.10 ORNAMENTAL METAL				
Railings, vertical square bars, 6" o.c., with shaped top rails				
Steel	L.F.	31.20	14.30	45.50
Aluminum	"	48.50	14.30	62.80
Bronze	"	89.00	19.05	108.05
Stainless steel	"	74.00	19.05	93.05

06   WOOD AND PLASTICS

FASTENERS AND ADHESIVES	UNIT	MAT.	INST.	TOTAL
06050.10 ACCESSORIES				
Column/post base, cast aluminum				
4" x 4"	EA.	1.65	6.45	8.10
6" x 6"	"	3.75	6.45	10.20
Anchors				
Bolts, threaded two ends, with nuts and washers				
1/2" dia.				
4" long	EA.	0.75	1.60	2.35
7-1/2" long	"	0.92	1.60	2.52
15" long	"	1.60	1.60	3.20
Bolts, carriage				
1/4 x 4	EA.	0.87	2.55	3.42
5/16 x 6	"	0.92	2.70	3.62
Joist and beam hangers				
18 ga.				
2 x 4	EA.	0.41	2.55	2.96
2 x 6	"	0.46	2.55	3.01
2 x 8	"	0.52	2.55	3.07
2 x 10	"	0.66	2.85	3.51
2 x 12	"	0.71	3.20	3.91
Sill anchors				
Embedded in concrete	EA.	5.30	2.55	7.85
Strap ties, 14 ga., 1-3/8" wide				
12" long	EA.	0.23	2.15	2.38
06110.30 FLOOR FRAMING				
Floor joists				
12" o.c.				
2x6	S.F.	0.50	0.51	1.01
2x8	"	0.69	0.52	1.21
2x10	"	1.00	0.54	1.54
2x12	"	1.30	0.56	1.86
3x6	"	1.20	0.55	1.75
3x8	"	1.55	0.56	2.11
3x10	"	1.95	0.58	2.53
16" o.c.				
2x6	S.F.	0.42	0.43	0.85
2x8	"	0.58	0.44	1.02
2x10	"	0.85	0.44	1.29
2x12	"	1.10	0.46	1.56
3x6	"	0.99	0.44	1.43
3x8	"	1.30	0.46	1.76
3x10	"	1.65	0.48	2.13
Sister joists for floors				
2x4	L.F.	0.28	1.60	1.88
2x6	"	0.38	1.85	2.23
2x8	"	0.58	2.15	2.73
2x10	"	0.85	2.55	3.40
2x12	"	1.10	3.20	4.30

FASTENERS AND ADHESIVES	UNIT	MAT.	INST.	TOTAL
06110.40 **FURRING**				
Furring, wood strips				
On masonry or concrete walls				
12" o.c.	S.F.	0.14	0.80	0.94
16" o.c.	"	0.12	0.73	0.85
24" o.c.	"	0.09	0.68	0.77
On wood walls				
12" o.c.	S.F.	0.14	0.57	0.71
16" o.c.	"	0.12	0.51	0.63
24" o.c.	"	0.09	0.47	0.56
Ceilings				
On masonry or concrete ceilings				
12" o.c.	S.F.	0.14	1.45	1.59
16" o.c.	"	0.12	1.30	1.42
24" o.c.	"	0.09	1.15	1.24
On wood ceilings				
12" o.c.	S.F.	0.14	0.95	1.09
16" o.c.	"	0.12	0.86	0.98
24" o.c.	"	0.09	0.78	0.87
06110.50 **ROOF FRAMING**				
Roof framing				
Rafters, gable end				
12" o.c.				
2x4	S.F.	0.33	0.54	0.87
2x6	"	0.50	0.56	1.06
2x8	"	0.69	0.58	1.27
2x10	"	1.00	0.61	1.61
2x12	"	1.30	0.64	1.94
16" o.c.				
2x6	S.F.	0.42	0.46	0.88
2x8	"	0.58	0.48	1.06
2x10	"	0.85	0.49	1.34
2x12	"	1.10	0.51	1.61
24" o.c.				
2x6	S.F.	0.33	0.39	0.72
2x8	"	0.46	0.40	0.86
2x10	"	0.68	0.41	1.09
2x12	"	0.88	0.43	1.31
Ridge boards				
2x6	L.F.	0.42	1.30	1.72
2x8	"	0.58	1.45	2.03
2x10	"	0.85	1.60	2.45
2x12	"	1.10	1.85	2.95
Hip rafters				
2x6	L.F.	0.42	0.92	1.34
2x8	"	0.58	0.95	1.53
2x10	"	0.85	0.99	1.84
2x12	"	1.10	1.05	2.15
Fascia boards				
2x4	L.F.	0.28	1.30	1.58
2x6	"	0.42	1.30	1.72
2x8	"	0.58	1.45	2.03

06   WOOD AND PLASTICS

FASTENERS AND ADHESIVES	UNIT	MAT.	INST.	TOTAL
06110.50 ROOF FRAMING				
2x10	L.F.	0.85	1.45	2.30
2x12	"	1.10	1.60	2.70
Cant strips				
3x3	L.F.	0.18	0.73	0.91
4x4	"	0.23	0.78	1.01
06110.60 SLEEPERS				
Sleepers, over concrete				
12" o.c.				
1x2	S.F.	0.14	0.58	0.72
2x4	"	0.33	0.71	1.04
06110.65 SOFFITS				
Soffit framing				
2x3	L.F.	0.21	1.85	2.06
2x4	"	0.28	2.00	2.28
2x6	"	0.42	2.15	2.57
2x8	"	0.58	2.35	2.93
06110.70 WALL FRAMING				
Framing wall, studs				
12" o.c.				
2x3	S.F.	0.24	0.48	0.72
2x4	"	0.33	0.48	0.81
2x6	"	0.50	0.51	1.01
2x8	"	0.69	0.54	1.23
16" o.c.				
2x3	S.F.	0.21	0.40	0.61
2x4	"	0.28	0.40	0.68
2x6	"	0.42	0.43	0.85
2x8	"	0.58	0.44	1.02
24" o.c.				
2x4	S.F.	0.22	0.35	0.57
2x6	"	0.33	0.37	0.70
2x8	"	0.46	0.38	0.84
Plates, top or bottom				
2x3	L.F.	0.21	0.76	0.97
2x4	"	0.28	0.80	1.08
2x6	"	0.42	0.86	1.28
2x8	"	0.58	0.92	1.50
Headers, door or window				
2x6				
Single				
3' long	EA.	1.25	12.85	14.10
6' long	"	2.50	16.10	18.60
2x8				
Single				
4' long	EA.	2.30	16.10	18.40
8' long	"	4.60	19.80	24.40
2x10				

06 WOOD AND PLASTICS

FASTENERS AND ADHESIVES	UNIT	MAT.	INST.	TOTAL
06110.70 **WALL FRAMING**				
Single				
5' long	EA.	4.20	19.80	24.00
10' long	"	8.45	25.70	34.15
2x12				
Single				
6' long	EA.	6.50	19.80	26.30
12' long	"	13.00	25.70	38.70
06115.10 **FLOOR SHEATHING**				
Sub-flooring, plywood, CDX				
1/2" thick	S.F.	0.36	0.32	0.68
5/8" thick	"	0.44	0.37	0.81
3/4" thick	"	0.58	0.43	1.01
Underlayment				
Plywood				
3/8" thick	S.F.	0.32	0.32	0.64
1/2" thick	"	0.37	0.34	0.71
5/8" thick	"	0.44	0.37	0.81
3/4" thick	"	0.50	0.40	0.90
06115.20 **ROOF SHEATHING**				
Sheathing				
3/8" thick	S.F.	0.35	0.33	0.68
1/2" thick	"	0.36	0.34	0.70
5/8" thick	"	0.44	0.37	0.81
3/4" thick	"	0.58	0.40	0.98
06115.30 **WALL SHEATHING**				
Sheathing				
Plywood, CDX				
3/8" thick	S.F.	0.35	0.38	0.73
1/2" thick	"	0.36	0.40	0.76
5/8" thick	"	0.44	0.43	0.87
3/4" thick	"	0.58	0.47	1.05
06125.10 **WOOD DECKING**				
Decking, T&G solid				
Fir				
3" thick	S.F.	1.85	0.64	2.49
4" thick	"	2.00	0.69	2.69
Southern yellow pine				
3" thick	S.F.	1.90	0.73	2.63
4" thick	"	2.10	0.79	2.89
White pine				
3" thick	S.F.	2.50	0.64	3.14
4" thick	"	3.25	0.69	3.94

06 WOOD AND PLASTICS

FASTENERS AND ADHESIVES	UNIT	MAT.	INST.	TOTAL
06130.10 HEAVY TIMBER				
Mill framed structures				
Beams to 20' long				
Douglas fir				
6x8	L.F.	4.05	3.20	7.25
6x10	"	4.85	3.30	8.15
Southern yellow pine				
6x8	L.F.	3.80	3.20	7.00
6x10	"	4.75	3.30	8.05
Columns to 12' high				
6x6	L.F.	3.45	4.80	8.25
10x10	"	7.15	5.35	12.50
06190.20 WOOD TRUSSES				
Truss, fink, 2x4 members				
3-in-12 slope				
24' span	EA.	35.50	27.50	63.00
30' span	"	48.50	29.20	77.70

FINISH CARPENTRY	UNIT	MAT.	INST.	TOTAL
06200.10 FINISH CARPENTRY				
Casing				
11/16 x 2-1/2	L.F.	0.81	1.15	1.96
11/16 x 3-1/2	"	1.05	1.20	2.25
Half round				
1/2	L.F.	0.21	1.05	1.26
5/8	"	0.25	1.05	1.30
Railings, balusters				
1-1/4 x 2-1/4	L.F.	1.40	2.55	3.95
1-1/8 x 1-1/8	"	1.20	2.35	3.55
Stop				
5/8 x 1-5/8				
Colonial	L.F.	0.29	1.60	1.89
Ranch	"	0.26	1.60	1.86
Exterior trim, casing, select pine, 1x3	"	0.87	1.30	2.17
Cornices, white pine, #2 or better				
1x4	L.F.	0.44	1.30	1.74
1x8	"	0.81	1.50	2.31
Shelving, pine				
1x8	L.F.	0.81	2.00	2.81
1x12	"	1.45	2.15	3.60

FINISH CARPENTRY

	UNIT	MAT.	INST.	TOTAL
06220.10 MILLWORK				
Countertop, laminated plastic				
25" x 7/8"				
Minimum	L.F.	8.80	6.45	15.25
Average	"	16.15	8.55	24.70
Maximum	"	25.40	10.30	35.70
Base cabinets, 34-1/2" high, 24" deep, hardwood, no tops				
Minimum	L.F.	40.40	10.30	50.70
Average	"	52.00	12.85	64.85
Maximum	"	81.00	17.15	98.15
Wall cabinets				
Minimum	L.F.	28.90	8.55	37.45
Average	"	40.40	10.30	50.70
Maximum	"	75.00	12.85	87.85

ARCHITECTURAL WOODWORK

	UNIT	MAT.	INST.	TOTAL
06420.10 PANEL WORK				
Plywood unfinished, 1/4" thick				
Birch				
Natural	S.F.	0.91	0.86	1.77
Select	"	1.20	0.86	2.06
Knotty pine	"	1.20	0.86	2.06
Plywood, prefinished, 1/4" thick, premium grade				
Birch veneer	S.F.	1.50	1.05	2.55
Cherry veneer	"	1.60	1.05	2.65
06430.10 STAIRWORK				
Risers, 1x8, 42" wide				
White oak	EA.	11.55	12.85	24.40
Pine	"	8.20	12.85	21.05
Treads, 1-1/16" x 9-1/2" x 42"				
White oak	EA.	15.00	16.10	31.10
06440.10 COLUMNS				
Column, hollow, round				
12" diameter				
10' high	EA.	346.00	36.70	382.70
12' high	"	416.00	39.30	455.30
24" diameter				
16' high	EA.	1,850	55.00	1,905
18' high	"	2,180	58.00	2,238

07 THERMAL AND MOISTURE

MOISTURE PROTECTION	UNIT	MAT.	INST.	TOTAL
07100.10 WATERPROOFING				
Membrane waterproofing, elastomeric				
Neoprene				
1/32" thick	S.F.	0.85	0.82	1.67
1/16" thick	"	1.35	0.85	2.20
Plastic vapor barrier (polyethylene)				1.90
4 mil	S.F.	0.01	0.08	0.09
6 mil	"	0.02	0.08	0.10
Bituminous membrane waterproofing, asphalt felt, 15 lb.				
One ply	S.F.	0.28	0.51	0.79
Two ply	"	0.33	0.62	0.95
Three ply	"	0.44	0.73	1.17
Bentonite waterproofing, panels				
3/16" thick	S.F.	0.15	0.51	0.66
1/4" thick	"	0.90	0.51	1.41
07160.10 BITUMINOUS DAMPPROOFING				
Building paper, asphalt felt				
15 lb	S.F.	0.07	0.82	0.89
30 lb	"	0.11	0.85	0.96
Asphalt dampproofing, troweled, cold, primer plus				
1 coat	S.F.	0.44	0.68	1.12
2 coats	"	0.68	1.00	1.68
3 coats	"	1.00	1.25	2.25
07190.10 VAPOR BARRIERS				
Vapor barrier, polyethylene				
2 mil	S.F.	0.01	0.10	0.11
6 mil	"	0.02	0.10	0.12
8 mil	"	0.03	0.11	0.14

INSULATION	UNIT	MAT.	INST.	TOTAL
07210.10 BATT INSULATION				
Ceiling, fiberglass, unfaced				
3-1/2" thick, R11	S.F.	0.24	0.24	0.48
6" thick, R19	"	0.41	0.27	0.68
9" thick, R30	"	0.63	0.31	0.94
Crawl space, unfaced				
3-1/2" thick, R11	S.F.	0.24	0.31	0.55
6" thick, R19	"	0.41	0.34	0.75
9" thick, R30	"	0.63	0.37	1.00
Wall, fiberglass				
Paper backed				

THERMAL AND MOISTURE

INSULATION	UNIT	MAT.	INST.	TOTAL
07210.10 BATT INSULATION				
2" thick, R7	S.F.	0.17	0.21	0.38
3" thick, R8	"	0.18	0.23	0.41
4" thick, R11	"	0.20	0.24	0.44
Foil backed, 1 side				
2" thick, R7	S.F.	0.35	0.21	0.56
3" thick, R11	"	0.37	0.23	0.60
4" thick, R14	"	0.42	0.24	0.66
Unfaced				
2" thick, R7	S.F.	0.15	0.21	0.36
3" thick, R9	"	0.18	0.23	0.41
4" thick, R11	"	0.22	0.24	0.46
6" thick, R19	"	0.25	0.25	0.50
07210.20 BOARD INSULATION				
Insulation, rigid				
0.75" thick, R2.78	S.F.	0.22	0.19	0.41
1.06" thick, R4.17	"	0.44	0.19	0.63
Perlite board, roof				
1.00" thick, R2.78	S.F.	0.44	0.17	0.61
Rigid urethane				
1" thick, R6.67	S.F.	0.53	0.17	0.70
1.20" thick, R8.33	"	0.67	0.17	0.84
Polystyrene				
1.0" thick, R4.17	S.F.	0.56	0.17	0.73
1.5" thick, R6.26	"	0.92	0.18	1.10
07210.60 LOOSE FILL INSULATION				
Blown-in type				
5" thick, R11	S.F.	0.18	0.17	0.35
6" thick, R13	"	0.21	0.20	0.41
Poured type				
1" thick, R4	S.F.	0.12	0.13	0.25
2" thick, R8	"	0.23	0.15	0.38
4" thick, R16	"	0.46	0.20	0.66
07210.70 SPRAYED INSULATION				
Foam, sprayed on				
Polystyrene				
1" thick, R4	S.F.	0.38	0.20	0.58
2" thick, R8	"	0.71	0.27	0.98
Urethane				
1" thick, R7.7	S.F.	0.44	0.20	0.64
2" thick, R15.4	"	0.77	0.27	1.04

07 THERMAL AND MOISTURE

SHINGLES AND TILES	UNIT	MAT.	INST.	TOTAL
07310.10 **ASPHALT SHINGLES**				
Standard asphalt shingles, strip shingles				
210 lb/square	SQ.	34.70	25.00	59.70
240 lb/square	"	38.10	31.30	69.40
Roll roofing, mineral surface				
90 lb	SQ.	18.50	17.90	36.40
140 lb	"	31.20	25.00	56.20
07310.30 **METAL SHINGLES**				
Aluminum, .020" thick				
Plain	SQ.	116.00	50.00	166.00
Steel, galvanized				
Plain	SQ.	154.00	50.00	204.00
07310.60 **SLATE SHINGLES**				
Slate shingles				
Ribbon	SQ.	346.00	125.00	471.00
Clear	"	462.00	125.00	587.00
07310.70 **WOOD SHINGLES**				
Wood shingles, on roofs				
White cedar, #1 shingles				
4" exposure	SQ.	154.00	83.50	237.50
5" exposure	"	138.00	62.50	200.50
#2 shingles				
4" exposure	SQ.	110.00	83.50	193.50
5" exposure	"	93.50	62.50	156.00
Resquared and rebutted				
4" exposure	SQ.	138.00	83.50	221.50
5" exposure	"	116.00	62.50	178.50
07310.80 **WOOD SHAKES**				
Shakes, hand split, 24" red cedar, on roofs				
5" exposure	SQ.	107.00	125.00	232.00
7" exposure	"	99.00	100.00	199.00
9" exposure	"	88.00	83.50	171.50

ROOFING AND SIDING	UNIT	MAT.	INST.	TOTAL
07410.10 **MANUFACTURED ROOFS**				
Aluminum roof panels, for structural steel framing				
Corrugated				
Natural finish				
.024"	S.F.	1.10	0.63	1.73

07 THERMAL AND MOISTURE

ROOFING AND SIDING	UNIT	MAT.	INST.	TOTAL
07410.10 MANUFACTURED ROOFS				
.030"	S.F.	1.35	0.63	1.98
Painted finish				
.024"	S.F.	1.55	0.63	2.18
.030"	"	1.75	0.63	2.38
Steel roof panels, for structural steel framing				
Corrugated, painted				
18 ga.	S.F.	3.35	0.63	3.98
20 ga.	"	3.10	0.63	3.73
07460.10 METAL SIDING PANELS				
Aluminum siding panels				
Corrugated				
Plain natural finish				
.024"	S.F.	1.00	1.15	2.15
.032"	"	1.20	1.15	2.35
Painted finish				
.024"	S.F.	1.25	1.15	2.40
.032"	"	1.45	1.15	2.60
Steel siding panels				
Corrugated				
22 ga.	S.F.	2.65	1.90	4.55
24 ga.	"	2.45	1.90	4.35
07460.50 PLASTIC SIDING				
Horizontal vinyl siding, solid				
8" wide				
Standard	S.F.	0.65	0.99	1.64
Insulated	"	0.95	0.99	1.94
10" wide				
Standard	S.F.	0.71	0.92	1.63
Insulated	"	1.05	0.92	1.97
07460.60 PLYWOOD SIDING				
Texture 1-11, 5/8" thick				
Cedar	S.F.	1.10	0.92	2.02
Fir	"	0.58	0.92	1.50
Redwood	"	1.10	0.89	1.99
Southern Yellow Pine	"	0.65	0.92	1.57
07460.70 STEEL SIDING				
Ribbed, sheets, galvanized				
22 ga.	S.F.	1.30	1.15	2.45
24 ga.	"	1.10	1.15	2.25
Primed				
24 ga.	S.F.	1.55	1.15	2.70
26 ga.	"	0.97	1.15	2.12

ROOFING AND SIDING	UNIT	MAT.	INST.	TOTAL
07460.80 WOOD SIDING				
Beveled siding, cedar				
A grade				
1/2 x 6	S.F.	1.70	1.30	3.00
1/2 x 8	"	2.00	1.05	3.05
3/4 x 10	"	1.80	0.86	2.66
Board and batten				
Cedar				
1x8	S.F.	1.85	1.05	2.90
1x12	"	1.45	0.83	2.28
Pine				
1x8	S.F.	0.55	1.05	1.60
1x12	"	0.47	0.83	1.30
Redwood				
1x8	S.F.	2.55	1.05	3.60
1x12	"	2.10	0.83	2.93
Tongue and groove				
Cedar				
1x6	S.F.	2.35	1.35	3.70
1x10	"	2.10	1.20	3.30
Pine				
1x6	S.F.	0.66	1.35	2.01
1x10	"	0.55	1.20	1.75
Redwood				
1x6	S.F.	2.45	1.35	3.80
1x10	"	2.20	1.20	3.40

MEMBRANE ROOFING	UNIT	MAT.	INST.	TOTAL
07510.10 BUILT-UP ASPHALT ROOFING				
Built-up roofing, asphalt felt, including gravel				
2 ply	SQ.	25.40	62.50	87.90
3 ply	"	35.80	83.50	119.30
4 ply	"	47.40	100.00	147.40
Cant strip, 4" x 4"				
Treated wood	L.F.	1.15	0.72	1.87
Foamglass	"	0.32	0.63	0.95
New gravel for built-up roofing, 400 lb/sq	SQ.	17.35	50.00	67.35
07530.10 SINGLE-PLY ROOFING				
Elastic sheet roofing				
Neoprene, 1/16" thick	S.F.	0.89	0.31	1.20
PVC				
45 mil	S.F.	1.25	0.31	1.56

MEMBRANE ROOFING	UNIT	MAT.	INST.	TOTAL
07530.10 SINGLE-PLY ROOFING				
Flashing				
Pipe flashing, 90 mil thick				
1" pipe	EA.	12.10	6.25	18.35
Neoprene flashing, 60 mil thick strip				
6" wide	L.F.	0.85	2.10	2.95
12" wide	"	1.65	3.15	4.80

FLASHING AND SHEET METAL	UNIT	MAT.	INST.	TOTAL
07620.10 FLASHING AND TRIM				
Counter flashing				
Aluminum, .032"	S.F.	0.88	2.50	3.38
Stainless steel, .015"	"	2.65	2.50	5.15
Copper				
16 oz.	S.F.	2.40	2.50	4.90
Valley flashing				
Aluminum, .032"	S.F.	0.88	1.55	2.43
Stainless steel, .015	"	2.65	1.55	4.20
Copper				
16 oz.	S.F.	2.40	1.55	3.95
Base flashing				
Aluminum, .040"	S.F.	0.94	2.10	3.04
Stainless steel, .018"	"	2.65	2.10	4.75
Copper				
16 oz.	S.F.	2.40	2.10	4.50
Flashing and trim, aluminum				
.019" thick	S.F.	0.76	1.80	2.56
.032" thick	"	0.91	1.80	2.71
07620.20 GUTTERS AND DOWNSPOUTS				
Aluminum gutter and downspout				
Downspouts				
2" x 3"	L.F.	0.63	1.65	2.28
3" x 4"	"	0.84	1.80	2.64
4" x 5"	"	0.94	1.95	2.89
Round				
3" dia.	L.F.	1.20	1.65	2.85
4" dia.	"	1.85	1.80	3.65
Gutters, stock units				
4" wide	L.F.	1.05	2.65	3.70
5" wide	"	1.15	2.80	3.95

FLASHING AND SHEET METAL	UNIT	MAT.	INST.	TOTAL
07700.10 ROOFING SPECIALTIES				
Smoke vent, 48" x 48"				
Aluminum	EA.	431.00	62.50	493.50
Galvanized steel	"	417.00	62.50	479.50
Heat/smoke vent, 48" x 96"				
Aluminum	EA.	1,660	83.50	1,744
Galvanized steel	"	1,620	83.50	1,704
Ridge vent strips				
Mill finish	L.F.	2.30	1.65	3.95
Soffit vents				
Mill finish				
2-1/2" wide	L.F.	0.25	1.00	1.25
Roof hatches				
Steel, plain, primed				
2'6" x 3'0"	EA.	363.00	62.50	425.50
Galvanized steel				
2'6" x 3'0"	EA.	375.00	62.50	437.50
Aluminum				
2'6" x 3'0"	EA.	399.00	62.50	461.50
Gravity ventilators, with curb, base, damper and screen				
Wind driven spinner				
6" dia.	EA.	15.10	16.70	31.80
12" dia.	"	23.00	16.70	39.70

SKYLIGHTS	UNIT	MAT.	INST.	TOTAL
07810.10 PLASTIC SKYLIGHTS				
Single thickness, not including mounting curb				
2' x 4'	EA.	145.00	31.30	176.30
4' x 4'	"	232.00	41.70	273.70
Double thickness, not including mounting curb				
2' x 4'	EA.	184.00	31.30	215.30
4' x 4'	"	290.00	41.70	331.70

DOORS AND WINDOWS

METAL	UNIT	MAT.	INST.	TOTAL
08110.10 METAL DOORS				
Flush hollow metal, standard duty, 20 ga., 1-3/8"				
2-6 x 6-8	EA.	133.00	28.60	161.60
2-8 x 6-8	"	136.00	28.60	164.60
3-0 x 6-8	"	150.00	28.60	178.60
1-3/4"				
2-6 x 6-8	EA.	158.00	28.60	186.60
2-8 x 6-8	"	167.00	28.60	195.60
3-0 x 6-8	"	179.00	28.60	207.60
Heavy duty, 20 ga., unrated, 1-3/4"				
2-8 x 6-8	EA.	139.00	28.60	167.60
3-0 x 6-8	"	150.00	28.60	178.60
08110.40 METAL DOOR FRAMES				
Hollow metal, stock, 18 ga., 4-3/4" x 1-3/4"				
2-0 x 7-0	EA.	56.50	32.20	88.70
2-4 x 7-0	"	56.50	32.20	88.70
2-6 x 7-0	"	58.00	32.20	90.20
3-0 x 7-0	"	59.00	32.20	91.20
08120.10 ALUMINUM DOORS				
Aluminum doors, commercial				
Narrow stile				
2-6 x 7-0	EA.	343.00	143.00	486.00
3-0 x 7-0	"	345.00	143.00	488.00
3-6 x 7-0	"	359.00	143.00	502.00
Wide stile				
2-6 x 7-0	EA.	808.00	143.00	951.00
3-0 x 7-0	"	808.00	143.00	951.00
3-6 x 7-0	"	832.00	143.00	975.00

WOOD AND PLASTIC	UNIT	MAT.	INST.	TOTAL
08210.10 WOOD DOORS				
Solid core, 1-3/8" thick				
Birch faced				
2-4 x 6-8	EA.	99.00	32.20	131.20
2-6 x 6-8	"	105.00	32.20	137.20
2-8 x 6-8	"	110.00	32.20	142.20
3-0 x 6-8	"	114.00	32.20	146.20
Hollow core, 1-3/8" thick				
Lauan faced				

08 DOORS AND WINDOWS

WOOD AND PLASTIC	UNIT	MAT.	INST.	TOTAL
08210.10 WOOD DOORS				
2-4 x 6-8	EA.	32.60	32.20	64.80
2-6 x 6-8	"	35.00	32.20	67.20
2-8 x 6-8	"	37.30	32.20	69.50
3-0 x 6-8	"	39.60	32.20	71.80
Closet doors, 1-3/4" thick				
Bi-fold or bi-passing, includes frame and trim				
Paneled				
4-0 x 6-8	EA.	220.00	42.90	262.90
6-0 x 6-8	"	268.00	42.90	310.90
Louvered				
4-0 x 6-8	EA.	152.00	42.90	194.90
6-0 x 6-8	"	194.00	42.90	236.90
Flush				
4-0 x 6-8	EA.	134.00	42.90	176.90
6-0 x 6-8	"	163.00	42.90	205.90
Primed				
4-0 x 6-8	EA.	140.00	42.90	182.90
6-0 x 6-8	"	169.00	42.90	211.90
08210.90 WOOD FRAMES				
Frame, interior, pine				
2-6 x 6-8	EA.	24.25	36.70	60.95
2-8 x 6-8	"	25.40	36.70	62.10
3-0 x 6-8	"	25.40	36.70	62.10
5-0 x 6-8	"	27.60	36.70	64.30
6-0 x 6-8	"	28.90	36.70	65.60
08300.10 SPECIAL DOORS				
Garage door, flush insulated metal, primed, 9-0 x 7-0	EA.	572.00	85.50	657.50
Roll-up doors				
13-0 high x 14-0 wide	EA.	700.00	367.00	1,067
12-0 high x 14-0 wide	"	898.00	367.00	1,265
Accordion folding doors, tracks and fittings included				
Vinyl covered, 2 layers	S.F.	7.35	10.30	17.65
Woven mahogany and vinyl	"	9.20	10.30	19.50
Economy vinyl	"	6.15	10.30	16.45
Rigid polyvinyl chloride	"	9.80	10.30	20.10
Sectional wood overhead doors, frames not included				
Commercial grade, heavy duty, 1-3/4" thick, manual				
8' x 8'	EA.	496.00	214.00	710.00
10' x 10'	"	770.00	234.00	1,004
12' x 12'	"	1,040	257.00	1,297
Sectional metal overhead doors, complete				
Residential grade, manual				
9' x 7'	EA.	280.00	103.00	383.00
16' x 7'	"	630.00	129.00	759.00
Sliding glass doors				
Tempered plate glass, 1/4" thick				
6' wide				
Economy grade	EA.	583.00	85.50	668.50
Premium grade	"	676.00	85.50	761.50
Insulating glass, 5/8" thick				

WOOD AND PLASTIC	UNIT	MAT.	INST.	TOTAL
08300.10 SPECIAL DOORS				
6' wide				
Economy grade	EA.	816.00	85.50	901.50
Premium grade	"	1,520	85.50	1,606

STOREFRONTS	UNIT	MAT.	INST.	TOTAL
08410.10 STOREFRONTS				
Storefront, aluminum and glass				
Minimum	S.F.	13.85	3.55	17.40
Average	"	18.50	4.10	22.60
Maximum	"	25.40	4.75	30.15
08520.10 ALUMINUM WINDOWS				
Fixed window				
6 sf to 8 sf	S.F.	8.10	4.10	12.20
12 sf to 16 sf	"	7.50	3.15	10.65
Projecting window				
6 sf to 8 sf	S.F.	18.50	7.15	25.65
12 sf to 16 sf	"	16.15	4.75	20.90
Horizontal sliding				
6 sf to 8 sf	S.F.	12.70	3.55	16.25
12 sf to 16 sf	"	11.55	2.85	14.40
Double hung				
6 sf to 8 sf	S.F.	11.55	5.70	17.25
10 sf to 12 sf	"	11.00	4.75	15.75
Storm window, 0.5 cfm, up to				
60 u.i. (united inches)	EA.	41.60	14.30	55.90
70 u.i.	"	42.70	14.30	57.00
80 u.i.	"	46.20	14.30	60.50

WOOD AND PLASTIC	UNIT	MAT.	INST.	TOTAL
08600.10 WOOD WINDOWS				
Double hung				
24" x 36"				

08 DOORS AND WINDOWS

WOOD AND PLASTIC	UNIT	MAT.	INST.	TOTAL
08600.10 WOOD WINDOWS				
Minimum	EA.	131.00	25.70	156.70
Average	"	187.00	32.20	219.20
Maximum	"	233.00	42.90	275.90
30" x 48"				
Minimum	EA.	187.00	28.60	215.60
Average	"	233.00	36.70	269.70
Maximum	"	280.00	51.50	331.50
Casement				
1 leaf, 22" x 38" high				
Minimum	EA.	187.00	25.70	212.70
Average	"	210.00	32.20	242.20
Maximum	"	233.00	42.90	275.90
2 leaf, 50" x 50" high				
Minimum	EA.	466.00	32.20	498.20
Average	"	560.00	42.90	602.90
Maximum	"	606.00	64.50	670.50
Picture window, fixed glass, 54" x 54" high				
Minimum	EA.	350.00	32.20	382.20
Average	"	437.00	36.70	473.70
Maximum	"	595.00	42.90	637.90
Sliding, 40" x 31" high				
Minimum	EA.	163.00	25.70	188.70
Average	"	257.00	32.20	289.20
Maximum	"	303.00	42.90	345.90
Awning windows				
34" x 21" high				
Minimum	EA.	173.00	25.70	198.70
Average	"	198.00	32.20	230.20
Maximum	"	245.00	42.90	287.90
40" x 21" high				
Minimum	EA.	204.00	28.60	232.60
Average	"	222.00	36.70	258.70
Maximum	"	268.00	51.50	319.50

HARDWARE	UNIT	MAT.	INST.	TOTAL
08710.10 HINGES				
Hinges				
3 x 3 butts, steel, interior, plain bearing	PAIR			11.00
4 x 4 butts, steel, standard	"			16.50
5 x 4-1/2 butts, bronze/s. steel, heavy duty	"			44.00

HARDWARE	UNIT	MAT.	INST.	TOTAL
08710.20 LOCKSETS				
Latchset, heavy duty				
Cylindrical	EA.	90.50	16.10	106.60
Mortise	"	81.50	25.70	107.20
Lockset, heavy duty				
Cylindrical	EA.	113.00	16.10	129.10
Mortise	"	131.00	25.70	156.70
08710.30 CLOSERS				
Door closers				
Standard	EA.	100.00	32.20	132.20
Heavy duty	"	111.00	32.20	143.20
08710.40 DOOR TRIM				
Panic device, unlabeled, rim type	EA.	373.00	64.50	437.50
Mortise	"	472.00	64.50	536.50
Vertical rod	"	548.00	64.50	612.50
Labeled, rim type	"	490.00	64.50	554.50
Mortise	"	589.00	64.50	653.50
Vertical rod	"	665.00	64.50	729.50
Door plates				
Kick plate, .050" aluminum, 3 beveled edges				
10" x 30"	EA.	11.65	12.85	24.50
10" x 34"	"	12.85	12.85	25.70
10" x 38"	"	14.00	12.85	26.85
Push plate, 4" x 16", .050"				
Aluminum	EA.	3.50	5.15	8.65
Bronze	"	7.00	5.15	12.15
Stainless steel	"	5.25	5.15	10.40
08710.60 WEATHERSTRIPPING				
Weatherstrip, head and jamb, metal strip, neoprene bulb				
Standard duty	L.F.	2.30	1.45	3.75
Heavy duty	"	3.00	1.60	4.60
Thresholds				
Bronze	L.F.	18.50	6.45	24.95
Aluminum				
Plain	L.F.	6.95	6.45	13.40
Vinyl insert	"	13.85	6.45	20.30
Aluminum with grit	"	12.15	6.45	18.60
Steel				
Plain	L.F.	9.25	6.45	15.70
Interlocking	"	14.45	21.45	35.90

08 DOORS AND WINDOWS

GLAZING	UNIT	MAT.	INST.	TOTAL
08810.10 GLAZING				
Sheet glass, 1/8" thick	S.F.	4.35	1.60	5.95
Plate glass, bronze or grey, 1/4" thick	"	6.45	2.60	9.05
Clear	"	4.95	2.60	7.55
Polished	"	5.50	2.60	8.10
Plexiglass				
1/8" thick	S.F.	1.75	2.60	4.35
1/4" thick	"	3.45	1.60	5.05
Clear, float glass				
3/16" thick	S.F.	3.35	2.40	5.75
1/4" thick	"	4.30	2.60	6.90
3/8" thick	"	7.75	3.55	11.30
Tinted glass, polished plate, twin ground				
3/16" thick	S.F.	3.60	2.40	6.00
1/4" thick	"	4.50	2.60	7.10
3/8" thick	"	8.00	3.55	11.55
Insulating glass, two lites, clear float glass				
1/2" thick	S.F.	7.20	4.75	11.95
5/8" thick	"	8.30	5.70	14.00
3/4" thick	"	9.15	7.15	16.30
7/8" thick	"	9.60	8.15	17.75
1" thick	"	10.30	9.50	19.80
Plate mirror glass				
Wall type, 1/4" thick				
15 sf	S.F.	7.30	2.85	10.15
Over 15 sf	"	6.70	2.60	9.30

SUPPORT SYSTEMS	UNIT	MAT.	INST.	TOTAL
09110.10 METAL STUDS				
Studs, non load bearing, galvanized				
2-1/2", 20 ga.				
12" o.c.	S.F.	0.48	0.54	1.02
16" o.c.	"	0.41	0.43	0.84
25 ga.				
12" o.c.	S.F.	0.35	0.54	0.89
16" o.c.	"	0.25	0.43	0.68
24" o.c.	"	0.19	0.36	0.55
3-5/8", 20 ga.				
12" o.c.	S.F.	0.51	0.64	1.15
16" o.c.	"	0.48	0.51	0.99
24" o.c.	"	0.43	0.43	0.86
25 ga.				
12" o.c.	S.F.	0.31	0.64	0.95
16" o.c.	"	0.26	0.51	0.77
24" o.c.	"	0.24	0.43	0.67
4", 20 ga.				
12" o.c.	S.F.	0.67	0.64	1.31
16" o.c.	"	0.57	0.51	1.08
24" o.c.	"	0.48	0.43	0.91
25 ga.				
12" o.c.	S.F.	0.36	0.64	1.00
16" o.c.	"	0.34	0.51	0.85
24" o.c.	"	0.28	0.43	0.71
6", 20 ga.				
12" o.c.	S.F.	0.81	0.80	1.61
16" o.c.	"	0.69	0.64	1.33
24" o.c.	"	0.57	0.54	1.11
25 ga.				
12" o.c.	S.F.	0.45	0.80	1.25
16" o.c.	"	0.41	0.64	1.05
24" o.c.	"	0.36	0.54	0.90
Load bearing studs, galvanized				
3-5/8", 16 ga.				
12" o.c.	S.F.	1.35	0.64	1.99
16" o.c.	"	1.25	0.51	1.76
18 ga.				
12" o.c.	S.F.	1.15	0.43	1.58
16" o.c.	"	1.05	0.51	1.56
4", 16 ga.				
12" o.c.	S.F.	1.50	0.64	2.14
16" o.c.	"	1.20	0.51	1.71
6", 16 ga.				
12" o.c.	S.F.	1.60	0.80	2.40
16" o.c.	"	1.50	0.64	2.14
Furring, 16" o.c.				
Installed on solid walls				
3/4" channels	S.F.	0.32	0.99	1.31
1-1/2" channels	"	0.52	1.05	1.57
Installed on columns and beams				
7/8" channel	L.F.	0.31	1.70	2.01
1-5/8" channel	"	0.52	1.70	2.22

SUPPORT SYSTEMS	UNIT	MAT.	INST.	TOTAL
09110.10 METAL STUDS				
Furring on ceilings				
3/4" furring channels				
12" o.c.	S.F.	0.35	1.85	2.20
16" o.c.	"	0.29	1.70	1.99
1-1/2" furring channels, 24" o.c.	"	0.25	1.45	1.70

LATH AND PLASTER	UNIT	MAT.	INST.	TOTAL
09205.10 GYPSUM LATH				
Gypsum lath, 1/2" thick				
Clipped	S.Y.	4.40	1.45	5.85
Nailed	"	4.05	1.60	5.65
09205.20 METAL LATH				
Stucco lath				
1.8 lb.	S.Y.	2.90	3.20	6.10
3.6 lb.	"	3.30	3.20	6.50
Paper backed				
Minimum	S.Y.	3.40	2.55	5.95
Maximum	"	3.85	3.65	7.50
09210.10 PLASTER				
Gypsum plaster, trowel finish, 2 coats				
Ceilings	S.Y.	3.65	6.10	9.75
Walls	"	3.65	5.65	9.30
3 coats				
Ceilings	S.Y.	5.05	8.50	13.55
Walls	"	5.05	7.30	12.35
09220.10 PORTLAND CEMENT PLASTER				
Stucco, portland, gray, 3 coat, 1" thick				
Sand finish	S.Y.	3.80	11.10	14.90
Trowel finish	"	3.80	11.60	15.40
White cement				
Sand finish	S.Y.	4.35	11.60	15.95
Trowel finish	"	4.35	12.75	17.10
Scratch coat				
For ceramic tile	S.Y.	1.35	2.55	3.90
For quarry tile	"	1.35	2.55	3.90
Portland cement plaster				
2 coats, 1/2"	S.F.	0.26	0.57	0.83
3 coats, 7/8"	"	0.36	0.73	1.09

LATH AND PLASTER	UNIT	MAT.	INST.	TOTAL
09250.10 GYPSUM BOARD				
Drywall, plasterboard, 3/8" clipped to				
Metal furred ceiling	S.F.	0.25	0.29	0.54
Columns and beams	"	0.25	0.64	0.89
Walls	"	0.25	0.26	0.51
Nailed or screwed to				
Wood framed ceiling	S.F.	0.25	0.26	0.51
Columns and beams	"	0.25	0.57	0.82
Walls	"	0.25	0.23	0.48
1/2", clipped to				
Metal furred ceiling	S.F.	0.31	0.29	0.60
Columns and beams	"	0.31	0.64	0.95
Walls	"	0.31	0.26	0.57
Nailed or screwed to				
Wood framed ceiling	S.F.	0.31	0.26	0.57
Columns and beams	"	0.31	0.57	0.88
Walls	"	0.31	0.23	0.54
5/8", clipped to				
Metal furred ceiling	S.F.	0.34	0.32	0.66
Columns and beams	"	0.34	0.71	1.05
Walls	"	0.34	0.29	0.63
Nailed or screwed to				
Wood framed ceiling	S.F.	0.34	0.32	0.66
Columns and beams	"	0.34	0.71	1.05
Walls	"	0.34	0.29	0.63
Taping and finishing joints	"	0.03	0.17	0.20

TILE	UNIT	MAT.	INST.	TOTAL
09310.10 CERAMIC TILE				
Glazed wall tile, 4-1/4" x 4-1/4"				
Minimum	S.F.	1.50	1.80	3.30
Average	"	2.35	2.10	4.45
Maximum	"	6.15	2.50	8.65
Unglazed floor tile				
Portland cement bed, cushion edge, face mounted				
1" x 1"	S.F.	4.55	2.30	6.85
1" x 2"	"	7.30	2.20	9.50
2" x 2"	"	4.80	2.10	6.90
Adhesive bed, with white grout				
1" x 1"	S.F.	4.05	2.30	6.35
1" x 2"	"	4.15	2.20	6.35
2" x 2"	"	4.20	2.10	6.30

09 FINISHES

TILE	UNIT	MAT.	INST.	TOTAL
09330.10 QUARRY TILE				
Floor				
4 x 4 x 1/2"	S.F.	3.40	3.35	6.75
6 x 6 x 1/2"	"	3.45	3.15	6.60
6 x 6 x 3/4"	"	3.95	3.15	7.10
Wall, applied to 3/4" portland cement bed				
4 x 4 x 1/2"	S.F.	3.05	5.05	8.10
6 x 6 x 3/4"	"	3.80	4.20	8.00
Cove base				
5 x 6 x 1/2" straight top	L.F.	2.95	4.20	7.15
6 x 6 x 3/4" round top	"	3.15	4.20	7.35
09410.10 TERRAZZO				
Floors bonded to concrete, 1-3/4" thick, 5/8" topping				
Gray cement	S.F.	2.60	3.65	6.25
White cement	"	2.85	3.65	6.50
Not bonded, 3" thick, 5/8" top, 1/4" sand cushion				
Gray cement	S.F.	3.10	4.25	7.35
White cement	"	3.45	4.25	7.70
Monolithic terrazzo, 3-1/2" base slab, 5/8" topping	"	2.20	3.20	5.40
Terrazzo tiles, non-slip surface				
9" x 9" x 1" thick	S.F.	9.75	3.65	13.40
12" x 12"				
1" thick	S.F.	10.70	3.40	14.10
1-1/2" thick	"	11.15	3.65	14.80
18" x 18" x 1-1/2" thick	"	14.50	3.65	18.15
24" x 24" x 1-1/2" thick	"	18.90	3.00	21.90

ACOUSTICAL TREATMENT	UNIT	MAT.	INST.	TOTAL
09510.10 CEILINGS AND WALLS				
Acoustical panels, suspension system not included				
Fiberglass panels				
5/8" thick				
2' x 2'	S.F.	0.54	0.29	0.83
2' x 4'	"	0.54	0.26	0.80
3/4" thick				
2' x 2'	S.F.	0.79	0.29	1.08
2' x 4'	"	0.79	0.26	1.05
Mineral fiber panels				
5/8" thick				
2' x 2'	S.F.	0.59	0.29	0.88
2' x 4'	"	0.59	0.26	0.85
3/4" thick				
2' x 2'	S.F.	0.74	0.29	1.03

09 FINISHES

ACOUSTICAL TREATMENT	UNIT	MAT.	INST.	TOTAL
09510.10 CEILINGS AND WALLS				
2' x 4'	S.F.	0.74	0.26	1.00
Ceiling suspension systems				
T bar system				
2' x 4'	S.F.	1.25	0.26	1.51
2' x 2'	"	1.45	0.29	1.74

FLOORING	UNIT	MAT.	INST.	TOTAL
09550.10 WOOD FLOORING				
Wood strip flooring, unfinished				
Fir floor				
C and better				
Vertical grain	S.F.	2.00	0.86	2.86
Flat grain	"	1.90	0.86	2.76
Oak floor				
Minimum	S.F.	2.45	1.20	3.65
Maximum	"	3.45	1.20	4.65
Maple floor				
Minimum	S.F.	2.35	1.20	3.55
Maximum	"	2.95	1.20	4.15
Parquet, 5/16", white oak				
Finished	S.F.	5.60	1.30	6.90
Unfinished	"	1.85	1.30	3.15
Finishing, sand, fill, finish, and wax	"	0.41	0.64	1.05
Refinish sand, seal, and 2 coats of polyurethane	"	0.71	0.86	1.57
Clean and wax floors	"	0.12	0.13	0.25
09630.10 UNIT MASONRY FLOORING				
Clay brick				
9 x 4-1/2 x 3" thick				
Glazed	S.F.	4.80	2.15	6.95
Unglazed	"	4.75	2.15	6.90
8 x 4 x 3/4" thick				
Glazed	S.F.	4.75	2.25	7.00
Unglazed	"	4.70	2.25	6.95
09660.10 RESILIENT TILE FLOORING				
Solid vinyl tile, 1/8" thick, 12" x 12"				
Marble patterns	S.F.	1.85	0.64	2.49
Solid colors	"	1.90	0.64	2.54
Travertine patterns	"	2.30	0.64	2.94

09 FINISHES

FLOORING	UNIT	MAT.	INST.	TOTAL
09665.10 RESILIENT SHEET FLOORING				
Vinyl sheet flooring				
Minimum	S.F.	2.10	0.26	2.36
Average	"	2.60	0.31	2.91
Maximum	"	4.60	0.43	5.03
Cove, to 6"	L.F.	0.58	0.51	1.09
09682.10 CARPET PADDING				
Carpet padding				
Foam rubber, waffle type, 0.3" thick	S.Y.	3.65	1.30	4.95
Jute padding				
Minimum	S.Y.	2.65	1.15	3.80
Average	"	3.20	1.30	4.50
Maximum	"	3.95	1.45	5.40
Sponge rubber cushion				
Minimum	S.Y.	3.30	1.15	4.45
Average	"	3.50	1.30	4.80
Maximum	"	3.75	1.45	5.20
Urethane cushion, 3/8" thick				
Minimum	S.Y.	2.10	1.15	3.25
Average	"	2.40	1.30	3.70
Maximum	"	2.65	1.45	4.10
09685.10 CARPET				
Carpet, acrylic				
24 oz., light traffic	S.Y.	17.35	1.45	18.80
28 oz., medium traffic	"	21.95	1.45	23.40
Residential				
Nylon				
15 oz., light traffic	S.Y.	12.45	1.45	13.90
28 oz., medium traffic	"	14.95	1.45	16.40
Commercial				
Nylon				
28 oz., medium traffic	S.Y.	15.95	1.45	17.40
35 oz., heavy traffic	"	19.05	1.45	20.50
Wool				
30 oz., medium traffic	S.Y.	26.00	1.45	27.45
36 oz., medium traffic	"	27.40	1.45	28.85
42 oz., heavy traffic	"	29.90	1.45	31.35
Carpet tile				
Foam backed	S.F.	2.30	0.26	2.56
Tufted loop or shag	"	2.55	0.26	2.81
Clean and vacuum carpet				
Minimum	S.Y.	0.18	0.10	0.28
Average	"	0.29	0.17	0.46
Maximum	"	0.35	0.26	0.61
09700.10 SPECIAL FLOORING				
Epoxy flooring, marble chips				
Epoxy with colored quartz chips in 1/4" base	S.F.	6.35	1.45	7.80
Heavy duty epoxy topping, 3/16" thick	"	5.50	1.45	6.95

PAINTING	UNIT	MAT.	INST.	TOTAL
09910.10 **EXTERIOR PAINTING**				
Exterior painting				
Wood surfaces, 1 coat primer, two coats paint				
Door and frame	EA.	3.05	43.70	46.75
Windows	S.F.	0.06	0.65	0.71
Wood trim	"	0.14	0.65	0.79
Wood siding	"	0.14	0.33	0.47
Hardboard surfaces				
One coat primer, two coats paint	S.F.	0.14	0.33	0.47
Asbestos cement surfaces				
One coat primer, two coats paint	S.F.	0.17	0.33	0.50
Galvanized surfaces, galvanized primer				
One coat primer, two coats paint	S.F.	0.15	0.31	0.46
Stucco surfaces, acrylic primer, acrylic latex paint				
One coat primer, two coats paint	S.F.	0.15	0.44	0.59
Concrete masonry unit surfaces, brush work				
One coat filler, one coat paint	S.F.	0.18	0.33	0.51
Two coats epoxy	"	0.25	0.44	0.69
Texture coating	"	0.23	0.26	0.49
Concrete surfaces				
One coat filler, one coat paint	S.F.	0.14	0.33	0.47
Two coats paint	"	0.21	0.44	0.65
Structural steel				
One field coat paint, brush work				
Light framing	S.F.	0.08	0.22	0.30
Heavy framing	"	0.08	0.13	0.21
Pipes, one coat primer, one coat paint				
4" dia.	L.F.	0.06	0.33	0.39
8" dia.	"	0.14	0.44	0.58
12" dia.	"	0.26	0.65	0.91
Miscellaneous surfaces				
Stair pipe rails				
Two rails	L.F.	0.12	0.87	0.99
One rail	"	0.07	0.52	0.59
Stair to 4' wide, including rails, per riser	EA.	0.53	3.75	4.28
Gratings and frames	S.F.	0.12	0.87	0.99
Ladders	L.F.	0.14	0.75	0.89
09920.10 **INTERIOR PAINTING**				
Walls, concrete and masonry, brush, primer, acrylic				
One coat primer, one coat paint	S.F.	0.08	0.33	0.41
Two coats paint	"	0.12	0.44	0.56
Plywood, paint	"	0.04	0.15	0.19
Natural finish	"	0.06	0.16	0.22
Wood, paint	"	0.06	0.16	0.22
Natural finish	"	0.07	0.19	0.26
Metal				
One coat filler	S.F.	0.12	0.16	0.28
One coat primer, one coat paint	"	0.14	0.33	0.47
Two coats paint	"	0.19	0.44	0.63
Plaster or gypsum board, paint	"	0.07	0.15	0.22
Epoxy	"	0.09	0.16	0.25
Ceilings, one coat paint, wood	"	0.06	0.19	0.25

09 FINISHES

PAINTING	UNIT	MAT.	INST.	TOTAL
09920.10 INTERIOR PAINTING				
Concrete	S.F.	0.09	0.16	0.25
Plaster	"	0.06	0.15	0.21
09920.30 DOORS AND MILLWORK				
Painting, doors				
Minimum	S.F.	0.12	0.87	0.99
Average	"	0.18	1.30	1.48
Maximum	"	0.30	1.75	2.05
Cabinets, shelves, and millwork				
Minimum	S.F.	0.09	0.44	0.53
Average	"	0.12	0.75	0.87
Maximum	"	0.14	1.30	1.44
09920.60 WINDOWS				
Painting, windows				
Minimum	S.F.	0.06	0.52	0.58
Average	"	0.07	0.65	0.72
Maximum	"	0.09	1.05	1.14
09955.10 WALL COVERING				
Vinyl wall covering				
Medium duty	S.F.	0.85	0.37	1.22
Heavy duty	"	1.10	0.44	1.54
Cork wall covering				
1' x 1' squares				
1/4" thick	S.F.	1.20	0.65	1.85
1/2" thick	"	1.35	0.65	2.00
3/4" thick	"	1.50	0.65	2.15
Wall fabrics				
Natural fabrics, grass cloths				
Minimum	S.F.	0.70	0.40	1.10
Average	"	0.88	0.44	1.32
Maximum	"	2.75	0.52	3.27
09980.10 PAINTING PREPARATION				
Cleaning, light				
Wood	S.F.	0.03	0.07	0.10
Plaster or gypsum wallboard	"	0.03	0.06	0.09
Normal painting prep, masonry and concrete				
Unpainted	S.F.	0.03	0.04	0.07
Painted	"	0.03	0.07	0.10
Plaster or gypsum				
Unpainted	S.F.	0.03	0.04	0.07
Painted	"	0.03	0.07	0.10
Wood				
Unpainted	S.F.	0.03	0.04	0.07
Painted	"	0.03	0.07	0.10
Sandblasting				
Brush off blast	S.F.	0.12	0.17	0.29
Commercial blast	"	0.23	0.44	0.67

09	FINISHES				

PAINTING		UNIT	MAT.	INST.	TOTAL
09980.10	PAINTING PREPARATION				
Near white metal blast		S.F.	0.33	0.75	1.08
White metal blast		"	0.44	0.87	1.31
09980.15	PAINT				
Paint, enamel					
600 sf per gal.		GAL			23.65
550 sf per gal.		"			18.25
500 sf per gal.		"			13.75
450 sf per gal.		"			12.65
350 sf per gal.		"			12.10
Latex, 400 sf per gal.		"			11.45
Aluminum					
400 sf per gal.		GAL			15.95
500 sf per gal.		"			30.80
Red lead, 350 sf per gal.		"			27.50
Primer					
400 sf per gal.		GAL			18.25
300 sf per gal.		"			18.15
Latex base, interior, white		"			15.20
Sealer and varnish					
400 sf per gal.		GAL			14.00
425 sf per gal.		"			20.50
600 sf per gal.		"			27.50

10 SPECIALTIES

SPECIALTIES	UNIT	MAT.	INST.	TOTAL
10210.10 VENTS AND WALL LOUVERS				
Vents w/screen, 4" deep, 8" wide, 5" high				
Modular	EA.	54.50	8.95	63.45
Aluminum gable louvers	S.F.	9.80	4.75	14.55
Vent screen aluminum, 4" wide, continuous	L.F.	2.60	0.95	3.55
Wall louver, aluminum mill finish				
Under, 2 sf	S.F.	20.20	3.55	23.75
2 to 4 sf	"	17.35	3.15	20.50
5 to 10 sf	"	16.45	3.15	19.60
Galvanized steel				
Under 2 sf	S.F.	19.65	3.55	23.20
2 to 4 sf	"	13.85	3.15	17.00
5 to 10 sf	"	13.00	3.15	16.15
10225.10 DOOR LOUVERS				
Fixed, 1" thick, enameled steel				
8"x8"	EA.	31.70	3.20	34.90
12"x8"	"	35.10	3.20	38.30
12"x12"	"	39.70	3.65	43.35
20"x8"	"	64.50	3.65	68.15
10520.10 FIRE PROTECTION				
Portable fire extinguishers				
Water pump tank type				
2.5 gal.				
Red enameled galvanized	EA.	71.50	13.60	85.10
Red enameled copper	"	81.00	13.60	94.60
Carbon dioxide type, red enamel steel				
Squeeze grip with hose and horn				
2.5 lb	EA.	37.90	13.60	51.50
5 lb	"	79.00	15.70	94.70
10 lb	"	114.00	20.40	134.40
Dry chemical, pressurized type				
Red enameled steel				
2.5 lb	EA.	17.85	13.60	31.45
5 lb	"	26.20	15.70	41.90
Fire extinguisher cabinets				
Enameled steel				
8" x 12" x 27"	EA.	114.00	40.80	154.80
8" x 16" x 38"	"	146.00	40.80	186.80
10550.10 POSTAL SPECIALTIES				
Residential postal accessories				
Letter slot	EA.	62.00	12.85	74.85
Rural letter box	"	42.50	32.20	74.70
Apartment house, keyed, 3.5" x 4.5" x 16"	"	62.00	8.55	70.55
10800.10 BATH ACCESSORIES				
Grab bar, 1-1/2" dia., stainless steel, wall mounted				
24" long	EA.	31.40	12.85	44.25
36" long	"	44.90	13.55	58.45

SPECIALTIES	UNIT	MAT.	INST.	TOTAL
10800.10 BATH ACCESSORIES				
1" dia., stainless steel				
12" long	EA.	24.70	11.20	35.90
24" long	"	29.20	12.85	42.05
36" long	"	37.00	14.30	51.30
Hand dryer, surface mounted, 110 volt	"	280.00	32.20	312.20
Medicine cabinet, 16 x 22, baked enamel, steel, lighted	"	56.00	10.30	66.30
With mirror, lighted	"	101.00	17.15	118.15
Mirror, 1/4" plate glass, up to 10 sf	S.F.	5.40	2.55	7.95
Mirror, stainless steel frame				
18"x24"	EA.	84.00	8.55	92.55
24"x30"	"	112.00	12.85	124.85
24"x60"	"	236.00	25.70	261.70
With shelf, 18"x24"	"	129.00	10.30	139.30
Sanitary napkin dispenser, stainless steel, wall mounted	"	309.00	17.15	326.15
Shower rod, 1" diameter				
Chrome finish over brass	EA.	50.50	12.85	63.35
Stainless steel	"	48.80	12.85	61.65
Toilet tissue dispenser, stainless, wall mounted				
Single roll	EA.	30.30	6.45	36.75
Double roll	"	47.10	7.35	54.45
Towel dispenser, stainless steel				
Flush mounted	EA.	140.00	14.30	154.30
Surface mounted	"	73.00	12.85	85.85
Combination towel dispenser and waste receptacle	"	275.00	17.15	292.15
Towel bar, stainless steel				
18" long	EA.	25.80	10.30	36.10
24" long	"	30.30	11.70	42.00
30" long	"	32.50	12.85	45.35
36" long	"	35.90	14.30	50.20
Toothbrush and tumbler holder	"	21.90	8.55	30.45
Waste receptacle, stainless steel, wall mounted	"	185.00	21.45	206.45

11 ARCHITECTURAL

EQUIPMENT	UNIT	MAT.	INST.	TOTAL
11450.10 RESIDENTIAL EQUIPMENT				
Compactor, 4 to 1 compaction	EA.	1,100	66.50	1,167
Dishwasher, built-in				
2 cycles	EA.	942.00	133.00	1,075
4 or more cycles	"	1,420	133.00	1,553
Disposal				
Garbage disposer	EA.	440.00	88.50	528.50
Heaters, electric, built-in				
Ceiling type	EA.	236.00	88.50	324.50
Wall type	"	148.00	88.50	236.50
1500 watt, wall type	"	167.00	66.50	233.50
3000 watt, wall type	"	275.00	88.50	363.50
Hood for range, 2-speed, vented				
30" wide	EA.	118.00	88.50	206.50
42" wide	"	516.00	88.50	604.50
Ice maker, automatic				
30 lb per day	EA.	752.00	37.90	789.90
50 lb per day	"	1,590	133.00	1,723
Folding access stairs, disappearing metal stair				
8' long	EA.	1,260	37.90	1,298
12' long	"	1,340	37.90	1,378
Wood frame, wood stair				
22" x 54" x 8'9" long	EA.	60.50	26.50	87.00
25" x 54" x 10' long	"	63.50	26.50	90.00
Ranges electric				
Free standing, 21", 1 oven	EA.	600.00	88.50	688.50
Built-in, 30", 1 oven	"	800.00	88.50	888.50
2 oven	"	1,200	88.50	1,289
Counter top, 4 burner, standard	"	752.00	66.50	818.50
With grill	"	1,590	66.50	1,657
Free standing 30", 1 oven	"	870.00	53.00	923.00
2 oven	"	2,500	53.00	2,553
Water softener				
30 grains per gallon	EA.	1,090	88.50	1,179
70 grains per gallon	"	1,500	133.00	1,633

12 FURNISHINGS

INTERIOR	UNIT	MAT.	INST.	TOTAL
12302.10 **CASEWORK**				
Kitchen base cabinet, prefinished, 24" deep, 35" high				
12"wide	EA.	108.00	25.70	133.70
24" wide	"	144.00	28.60	172.60
36" wide	"	196.00	32.20	228.20
48" wide	"	224.00	32.20	256.20
Corner cabinet, 36" wide	"	151.00	32.20	183.20
Wall cabinet, 12" deep, 12" high				
30" wide	EA.	86.00	25.70	111.70
36" wide	"	91.00	25.70	116.70
15" high				
30" wide	EA.	91.00	28.60	119.60
36" wide	"	98.50	28.60	127.10
24" high				
30" wide	EA.	108.00	28.60	136.60
36" wide	"	132.00	28.60	160.60
30" high				
12" wide	EA.	82.50	32.20	114.70
24" wide	"	101.00	32.20	133.20
36" wide	"	142.00	36.70	178.70
Corner cabinet, 30" high				
24" wide	EA.	132.00	42.90	174.90
36" wide	"	176.00	42.90	218.90
Vanity with top, laminated plastic				
30" wide	EA.	309.00	64.50	373.50
48" wide	"	372.00	103.00	475.00
12390.10 **COUNTER TOPS**				
Stainless steel, counter top, with backsplash	S.F.	66.00	6.45	72.45
Acid-proof, kemrock surface	"	17.60	4.30	21.90
12500.10 **WINDOW TREATMENT**				
Drapery tracks, wall or ceiling mounted				
Basic traverse rod				
50 to 90"	EA.	25.70	12.85	38.55
84 to 156"	"	39.50	14.30	53.80
12510.10 **BLINDS**				
Venetian blinds				
2" slats	S.F.	2.40	0.64	3.04
1" slats	"	4.75	0.64	5.39

15 MECHANICAL

BASIC MATERIALS	UNIT	MAT.	INST.	TOTAL
15120.10 BACKFLOW PREVENTERS				
Backflow preventer, flanged, cast iron, with valves				
3" pipe	EA.	1,560	143.00	1,703
4" pipe	"	2,250	159.00	2,409
15140.11 PIPE HANGERS, LIGHT				
A band, black iron				
1/2"	EA.	0.42	2.05	2.47
1"	"	0.53	2.10	2.63
1-1/4"	"	0.58	2.20	2.78
Copper				
1/2"	EA.	0.48	2.05	2.53
3/4"	"	0.48	2.10	2.58
1"	"	0.51	2.10	2.61
2 hole clips, galvanized				
3/4"	EA.	0.14	1.90	2.04
1"	"	0.17	1.95	2.12
PVC coated hangers, galvanized, 28 ga.				
1-1/2" x 12"	EA.	0.70	1.90	2.60
2" x 12"	"	0.78	2.05	2.83
Wire hook hangers				
Black wire, 1/2" x				
4"	EA.	0.15	1.45	1.60
6"	"	0.19	1.50	1.69
15290.10 DUCTWORK INSULATION				
Fiberglass duct insulation, plain blanket				
1-1/2" thick	S.F.	0.21	0.36	0.57
2" thick	"	0.25	0.48	0.73

PLUMBING	UNIT	MAT.	INST.	TOTAL
15410.05 C.I. PIPE, ABOVE GROUND				
No hub pipe				
1-1/2" pipe	L.F.	2.25	2.05	4.30
2" pipe	"	2.50	2.40	4.90
3" pipe	"	2.70	2.85	5.55
4" pipe	"	3.50	4.75	8.25
15410.10 COPPER PIPE				
Type "K" copper				
1/2"	L.F.	0.74	0.89	1.63

PLUMBING		UNIT	MAT.	INST.	TOTAL
15410.10	**COPPER PIPE**				
3/4"		L.F.	2.30	0.95	3.25
1"		"	3.10	1.00	4.10
DWV, copper					
1-1/4"		L.F.	5.00	1.20	6.20
1-1/2"		"	5.80	1.30	7.10
2"		"	8.15	1.45	9.60
3"		"	14.65	1.60	16.25
4"		"	25.50	1.80	27.30
15410.30	**PVC/CPVC PIPE**				
PVC schedule 40					
1/2" pipe		L.F.	0.68	1.20	1.88
3/4" pipe		"	0.86	1.30	2.16
1" pipe		"	1.25	1.45	2.70
1-1/4" pipe		"	1.30	1.60	2.90
1-1/2" pipe		"	1.40	1.80	3.20
2" pipe		"	1.85	2.05	3.90
2-1/2" pipe		"	3.30	2.40	5.70
3" pipe		"	3.75	2.85	6.60
4" pipe		"	5.25	3.55	8.80
15430.23	**CLEANOUTS**				
Cleanout, wall					
2"		EA.	51.00	19.05	70.05
3"		"	57.00	19.05	76.05
4"		"	76.00	23.80	99.80
15430.25	**HOSE BIBBS**				
Hose bibb					
1/2"		EA.	4.45	9.50	13.95
3/4"		"	4.70	9.50	14.20
15430.60	**VALVES**				
Gate valve, 125 lb, bronze, soldered					
1/2"		EA.	8.25	7.15	15.40
3/4"		"	11.10	7.15	18.25
Threaded					
1/2"					
3/4"					
Ball valve, bronze, 250 lb, threaded					
1/2"		EA.	6.75	11.40	18.15
3/4"		"	11.20	11.40	22.60
Radiator temp control valve, with control and sensor					
1/2" valve		EA.	51.50	17.85	69.35
1" valve		"	60.50	17.85	78.35
Solar water temperature regulating valve					
3/4"		EA.	265.00	23.80	288.80
1"		"	271.00	28.60	299.60

15 MECHANICAL

PLUMBING	UNIT	MAT.	INST.	TOTAL
15430.70 DRAINS, ROOF & FLOOR				
Floor drain, cast iron, with cast iron top				
2"	EA.	67.00	23.80	90.80
3"	"	67.00	23.80	90.80
4"	"	67.00	23.80	90.80
Roof drain, cast iron				
2"	EA.	196.00	23.80	219.80
3"	"	196.00	23.80	219.80
4"	"	196.00	23.80	219.80

PLUMBING FIXTURES	UNIT	MAT.	INST.	TOTAL
15440.10 BATHS				
Bath tub, 5' long				
Minimum	EA.	323.00	95.00	418.00
Average	"	681.00	143.00	824.00
Maximum	"	1,020	286.00	1,306
6' long				
Minimum	EA.	370.00	95.00	465.00
Average	"	716.00	143.00	859.00
Maximum	"	1,120	286.00	1,406
Square tub, whirlpool, 4'x4'				
Minimum	EA.	1,120	143.00	1,263
Average	"	1,390	286.00	1,676
Maximum	"	2,990	357.00	3,347
5'x5'				
Minimum	EA.	1,140	143.00	1,283
Average	"	1,620	286.00	1,906
Maximum	"	3,120	357.00	3,477
6'x6'				
Minimum	EA.	1,330	143.00	1,473
Average	"	1,820	286.00	2,106
Maximum	"	3,810	357.00	4,167
For trim and rough-in				
Minimum	EA.	98.00	95.00	193.00
Average	"	139.00	143.00	282.00
Maximum	"	202.00	286.00	488.00
15440.12 DISPOSALS & ACCESSORIES				
Continuous feed				
Minimum	EA.	43.90	57.00	100.90
Maximum	"	219.00	95.00	314.00
Batch feed, 1/2 hp				
Minimum	EA.	161.00	57.00	218.00
Maximum	"	260.00	95.00	355.00

MECHANICAL

PLUMBING FIXTURES	UNIT	MAT.	INST.	TOTAL
15440.15　　　　FAUCETS				
Kitchen				
Minimum	EA.	86.50	47.60	134.10
Average	"	139.00	57.00	196.00
Maximum	"	167.00	71.50	238.50
Bath				
Minimum	EA.	139.00	47.60	186.60
Average	"	203.00	57.00	260.00
Maximum	"	219.00	71.50	290.50
Lavatory, domestic				
Minimum	EA.	89.00	47.60	136.60
Average	"	185.00	57.00	242.00
Maximum	"	277.00	71.50	348.50
Shower				
Minimum	EA.	104.00	47.60	151.60
Average	"	185.00	57.00	242.00
Maximum	"	289.00	71.50	360.50
For trim and rough-in				
Minimum	EA.	46.20	57.00	103.20
Average	"	69.50	71.50	141.00
Maximum	"	104.00	143.00	247.00
15440.20　　　　LAVATORIES				
Lavatory, counter top, porcelain enamel on cast iron				
Minimum	EA.	113.00	57.00	170.00
Average	"	167.00	71.50	238.50
Maximum	"	243.00	95.00	338.00
Wall hung, china				
Minimum	EA.	127.00	57.00	184.00
Average	"	173.00	71.50	244.50
Maximum	"	462.00	95.00	557.00
For trim and rough-in				
Minimum	EA.	110.00	71.50	181.50
Average	"	133.00	95.00	228.00
Maximum	"	231.00	143.00	374.00
15440.30　　　　SHOWERS				
Shower, fiberglass, 36"x34"x84"				
Minimum	EA.	450.00	204.00	654.00
Average	"	624.00	286.00	910.00
Maximum	"	895.00	286.00	1,181
Steel, 1 piece, 36"x36"				
Minimum	EA.	416.00	204.00	620.00
Average	"	612.00	286.00	898.00
Maximum	"	705.00	286.00	991.00
Receptor, molded stone, 36"x36"				
Minimum	EA.	139.00	95.00	234.00
Average	"	225.00	143.00	368.00
Maximum	"	346.00	238.00	584.00
For trim and rough-in				
Minimum	EA.	106.00	130.00	236.00
Average	"	133.00	159.00	292.00
Maximum	"	162.00	286.00	448.00

MECHANICAL

PLUMBING FIXTURES	UNIT	MAT.	INST.	TOTAL
15440.40 SINKS				
Kitchen sink, single, stainless steel, single bowl				
Minimum	EA.	121.00	57.00	178.00
Average	"	162.00	71.50	233.50
Maximum	"	229.00	95.00	324.00
Double bowl				
Minimum	EA.	162.00	71.50	233.50
Average	"	185.00	95.00	280.00
Maximum	"	248.00	143.00	391.00
Porcelain enamel, cast iron, single bowl				
Minimum	EA.	122.00	57.00	179.00
Average	"	146.00	71.50	217.50
Maximum	"	200.00	95.00	295.00
Double bowl				
Minimum	EA.	167.00	71.50	238.50
Average	"	191.00	95.00	286.00
Maximum	"	254.00	143.00	397.00
Washing machine box				
Minimum	EA.	104.00	71.50	175.50
Average	"	139.00	95.00	234.00
Maximum	"	185.00	143.00	328.00
For trim and rough-in				
Minimum	EA.	162.00	95.00	257.00
Average	"	231.00	143.00	374.00
Maximum	"	289.00	190.00	479.00
15440.60 WATER CLOSETS				
Water closet flush tank, floor mounted				
Minimum	EA.	187.00	71.50	258.50
Average	"	420.00	95.00	515.00
Maximum	"	723.00	143.00	866.00
For trim and rough-in				
Minimum	EA.	99.00	71.50	170.50
Average	"	117.00	95.00	212.00
Maximum	"	146.00	143.00	289.00
15440.70 WATER HEATERS				
Water heater, electric				
10 gal	EA.	145.00	47.60	192.60
20 gal	"	187.00	57.00	244.00
30 gal	"	195.00	57.00	252.00
40 gal	"	197.00	57.00	254.00
Oil fired				
20 gal	EA.	605.00	143.00	748.00
50 gal	"	935.00	204.00	1,139

15 MECHANICAL

HEATING & VENTILATING

HEATING & VENTILATING	UNIT	MAT.	INST.	TOTAL
15555.10 BOILERS				
Cast iron, gas fired, hot water				
115 mbh	EA.	1,060	917.00	1,977
175 mbh	"	1,290	1,000	2,290
235 mbh	"	1,910	1,100	3,010
Electric, hot water				
115 mbh	EA.	3,120	550.00	3,670
175 mbh	"	3,700	550.00	4,250
235 mbh	"	4,390	550.00	4,940
Oil fired, hot water				
115 mbh	EA.	1,730	733.00	2,463
175 mbh	"	2,190	846.00	3,036
235 mbh	"	2,540	1,000	3,540
15610.10 FURNACES				
Electric, hot air				
40 mbh	EA.	520.00	143.00	663.00
60 mbh	"	606.00	150.00	756.00
80 mbh	"	664.00	159.00	823.00
100 mbh	"	901.00	168.00	1,069
125 mbh	"	993.00	173.00	1,166
Gas fired hot air				
40 mbh	EA.	520.00	143.00	663.00
60 mbh	"	549.00	150.00	699.00
80 mbh	"	635.00	159.00	794.00
100 mbh	"	664.00	168.00	832.00
125 mbh	"	722.00	173.00	895.00
Oil fired hot air				
40 mbh	EA.	635.00	143.00	778.00
60 mbh	"	791.00	150.00	941.00
80 mbh	"	866.00	159.00	1,025
100 mbh	"	1,010	168.00	1,178
125 mbh	"	1,130	173.00	1,303

REFRIGERATION

REFRIGERATION	UNIT	MAT.	INST.	TOTAL
15670.10 CONDENSING UNITS				
Air cooled condenser, single circuit				
3 ton	EA.	1,320	47.60	1,368
5 ton	"	2,200	47.60	2,248
With low ambient dampers				
3 ton	EA.	1,540	71.50	1,612
5 ton	"	2,420	71.50	2,492

15 MECHANICAL

REFRIGERATION	UNIT	MAT.	INST.	TOTAL
15780.20 ROOFTOP UNITS				
Packaged, single zone rooftop unit, with roof curb				
2 ton	EA.	1,240	286.00	1,526
3 ton	"	1,770	286.00	2,056
4 ton	"	2,350	357.00	2,707
15830.10 RADIATION UNITS				
Baseboard radiation unit				
1.7 mbh/lf	L.F.	39.90	11.40	51.30
2.1 mbh/lf	"	52.50	14.30	66.80
15830.70 UNIT HEATERS				
Steam unit heater, horizontal				
12,500 btuh, 200 cfm	EA.	185.00	47.60	232.60
17,000 btuh, 300 cfm	"	214.00	47.60	261.60

AIR HANDLING	UNIT	MAT.	INST.	TOTAL
15855.10 AIR HANDLING UNITS				
Air handling unit, medium pressure, single zone				
1500 cfm	EA.	1,980	178.00	2,158
3000 cfm	"	2,540	317.00	2,857
Rooftop air handling units				
4950 cfm	EA.	6,930	317.00	7,247
7370 cfm	"	7,840	408.00	8,248

AIR DISTRIBUTION	UNIT	MAT.	INST.	TOTAL
15890.10 METAL DUCTWORK				
Rectangular duct				
Galvanized steel				
Minimum	Lb.	2.95	2.60	5.55
Average	"	3.30	3.15	6.45
Maximum	"	4.60	4.75	9.35
Aluminum				

15 MECHANICAL

AIR DISTRIBUTION	UNIT	MAT.	INST.	TOTAL
15890.10 METAL DUCTWORK				
Minimum	Lb.	6.25	5.70	11.95
Average	"	7.25	7.15	14.40
Maximum	"	10.90	9.50	20.40
Fittings				
Minimum	EA.	2.65	9.50	12.15
Average	"	5.30	14.30	19.60
Maximum	"	13.20	28.60	41.80
15890.30 FLEXIBLE DUCTWORK				
Flexible duct, 1.25" fiberglass				
5" dia.	L.F.	1.15	1.45	2.60
6" dia.	"	1.20	1.60	2.80
15910.10 DAMPERS				
Horizontal parallel aluminum backdraft damper				
12" x 12"	EA.	28.90	7.15	36.05
16" x 16"	"	40.40	8.15	48.55
20" x 20"	"	52.00	10.20	62.20
15940.10 DIFFUSERS				
Ceiling diffusers, round, baked enamel finish				
6" dia.	EA.	28.90	9.50	38.40
8" dia.	"	34.70	11.90	46.60
Rectangular				
6x6"	EA.	23.10	9.50	32.60
9x9"	"	27.70	14.30	42.00
12x12"	"	42.70	14.30	57.00
15x15"	"	59.00	14.30	73.30
18x18"	"	81.00	14.30	95.30
15940.40 REGISTERS AND GRILLES				
Lay in flush mounted, perforated face, return				
6x6/24x24	EA.	24.25	11.40	35.65
8x8/24x24	"	24.25	11.40	35.65
9x9/24x24	"	24.25	11.40	35.65
10x10/24x24	"	24.25	11.40	35.65

16 ELECTRICAL

BASIC MATERIALS		UNIT	MAT.	INST.	TOTAL
16050.30	**BUS DUCT**				
Bus duct, 100a, plug-in					
10', 600v		EA.	154.00	91.50	245.50
With ground		"	204.00	140.00	344.00
10', 277/480v		"	198.00	91.50	289.50
With ground		"	243.00	140.00	383.00
16110.12	**CABLE TRAY**				
Cable tray, 6"		L.F.	9.75	1.95	11.70
Ventilated cover		"	3.95	1.00	4.95
Solid cover		"	3.10	1.00	4.10
16110.21	**ALUMINUM CONDUIT**				
Aluminum conduit					
1/2"		L.F.	0.76	1.00	1.76
3/4"		"	0.99	1.35	2.34
1"		"	1.00	1.65	2.65
16110.22	**EMT CONDUIT**				
EMT conduit					
1/2"		L.F.	0.17	1.00	1.17
3/4"		"	0.23	1.35	1.58
1"		"	0.37	1.65	2.02
16110.23	**FLEXIBLE CONDUIT**				
Flexible conduit, steel					
1/2		L.F.	0.19	1.00	1.19
3/4"		"	0.26	1.35	1.61
1"		"	0.53	1.35	1.88
16110.24	**GALVANIZED CONDUIT**				
Galvanized rigid steel conduit					
1/2"		L.F.	0.76	1.35	2.11
3/4"		"	0.95	1.65	2.60
1"		"	1.30	1.95	3.25
16110.25	**PLASTIC CONDUIT**				
PVC conduit, schedule 40					
1/2"		L.F.	0.20	1.00	1.20
3/4"		"	0.25	1.00	1.25
1"		"	0.37	1.35	1.72
16110.27	**PLASTIC COATED CONDUIT**				
Rigid steel conduit, plastic coated					
1/2"		L.F.	2.15	1.65	3.80
3/4"		"	2.50	1.95	4.45
1"		"	3.25	2.65	5.90

16 ELECTRICAL

BASIC MATERIALS	UNIT	MAT.	INST.	TOTAL
16110.28 **STEEL CONDUIT**				
Intermediate metal conduit (IMC)				
1/2"	L.F.	0.71	1.00	1.71
3/4"	"	0.85	1.35	2.20
1"	"	1.15	1.65	2.80
16110.80 **WIREWAYS**				
Wireway, hinge cover type				
2-1/2" x 2-1/2"				
1' section	EA.	7.50	5.10	12.60
2'	"	10.65	6.30	16.95
3'	"	14.45	8.30	22.75
16120.41 **ALUMINUM CONDUCTORS**				
Type XHHW, stranded aluminum, 600v				
#8	L.F.	0.11	0.17	0.28
#6	"	0.17	0.20	0.37
#4	"	0.22	0.27	0.49
16120.43 **COPPER CONDUCTORS**				
Copper conductors, type THW, solid				
#14	L.F.	0.04	0.13	0.17
#12	"	0.07	0.17	0.24
#10	"	0.09	0.20	0.29
Type "BX" solid armored cable				
#14/2	L.F.	0.32	0.83	1.15
#14/3	"	0.40	0.93	1.33
#14/4	"	0.54	1.00	1.54
#12/2	"	0.34	0.93	1.27
#12/3	"	0.50	1.00	1.50
#12/4	"	0.70	1.15	1.85
16120.45 **FLAT CONDUCTOR CABLE**				
Flat conductor cable, with shield, 3 conductor				
#12 awg	L.F.	3.40	1.95	5.35
#10 awg	"	4.00	1.95	5.95
16120.47 **NON-METALLIC SHEATHED CABLE**				
Non-metallic sheathed cable				
Type NM cable with ground				
#14/2	L.F.	0.12	0.50	0.62
#12/2	"	0.18	0.53	0.71
#10/2	"	0.29	0.59	0.88
#8/2	"	0.59	0.66	1.25
#6/2	"	0.88	0.83	1.71
#14/3	"	0.20	0.86	1.06
#12/3	"	0.29	0.88	1.17
#10/3	"	0.43	0.90	1.33
#8/3	"	0.91	0.91	1.82

BASIC MATERIALS	UNIT	MAT.	INST.	TOTAL
16120.47 NON-METALLIC SHEATHED CABLE				
#6/3	L.F.	1.25	0.93	2.18
#4/3	"	1.85	1.05	2.90
#2/3	"	2.75	1.15	3.90
16130.40 BOXES				
Round cast box, type SEH				
1/2"	EA.	12.70	11.55	24.25
3/4"	"	13.85	13.95	27.80
SEHC				
1/2"	EA.	15.95	11.55	27.50
3/4"	"	16.75	13.95	30.70
Rectangle, type FS, 2 gang boxes				
1/2"	EA.	11.55	11.55	23.10
3/4"	"	12.40	13.25	25.65
1"	"	13.65	16.60	30.25
Weatherproof cast aluminum boxes, 1 gang, 3 outlets				
1/2"	EA.	3.30	13.25	16.55
3/4"	"	3.60	16.60	20.20
2 gang, 3 outlets				
1/2"	EA.	6.30	16.60	22.90
3/4"	"	6.60	17.70	24.30
16130.45 EXPLOSION PROOF FITTINGS				
Flexible couplings with female unions				
1/2" x 18"	EA.	72.00	6.65	78.65
3/4" x 18"	"	91.00	9.15	100.15
1" x 18"	"	152.00	11.55	163.55
16130.60 PULL AND JUNCTION BOXES				
4"				
Octagon box	EA.	1.05	3.80	4.85
Box extension	"	1.50	1.95	3.45
Plaster ring	"	0.80	1.95	2.75
Cover blank	"	0.34	1.95	2.29
Square box	"	1.25	3.80	5.05
Box extension	"	1.35	1.95	3.30
Plaster ring	"	0.63	1.95	2.58
Cover blank	"	0.40	1.95	2.35
16130.65 PULL BOXES AND CABINETS				
Galvanized pull boxes, screw cover				
4x4x4	EA.	3.45	6.30	9.75
4x6x4	"	4.30	6.30	10.60
16130.80 RECEPTACLES				
125 volt, 20a, duplex, grounding type, standard grade	EA.	4.65	6.65	11.30
Ground fault interrupter type	"	36.00	9.80	45.80
250 volt, 20a, 2 pole, single receptacle, ground type	"	5.40	6.65	12.05

BASIC MATERIALS	UNIT	MAT.	INST.	TOTAL
16130.80 RECEPTACLES				
120/208v, 4 pole, single receptacle, twist lock				
20a	EA.	11.60	11.55	23.15
Dryer receptacle, 250v, 30a/50a, 3 wire	"	14.20	9.80	24.00
Clock receptacle, 2 pole, grounding type	"	5.95	6.65	12.60
16350.10 CIRCUIT BREAKERS				
Molded case, 240v, 15-60a, bolt-on				
1 pole	EA.	7.20	8.30	15.50
2 pole	"	16.00	11.55	27.55
70-100a, 2 pole	"	42.30	17.70	60.00
15-60a, 3 pole	"	52.00	13.25	65.25
70-100a, 3 pole	"	75.50	20.40	95.90
16395.10 GROUNDING				
Ground rods, copper clad, 1/2" x				
6'	EA.	6.30	22.10	28.40
8'	"	8.15	24.10	32.25

SERVICE AND DISTRIBUTION	UNIT	MAT.	INST.	TOTAL
16470.10 PANELBOARDS				
120/208v, flush, 3 ph., 4 wire, main only				
100a				
12 circuits	EA.	315.00	169.00	484.00
20 circuits	"	434.00	209.00	643.00
30 circuits	"	629.00	233.00	862.00
225a				
30 circuits	EA.	658.00	257.00	915.00
42 circuits	"	835.00	316.00	1,151

LIGHTING	UNIT	MAT.	INST.	TOTAL
16510.05 INTERIOR LIGHTING				
Recessed fluorescent fixtures, 2'x2'				
2 lamp	EA.	44.00	24.10	68.10

LIGHTING	UNIT	MAT.	INST.	TOTAL
16510.05 INTERIOR LIGHTING				
4 lamp	EA.	59.00	24.10	83.10
Surface mounted incandescent fixtures				
40w	EA.	40.00	22.10	62.10
75w	"	43.50	22.10	65.60
100w	"	51.50	22.10	73.60
Recessed incandescent fixtures				
40w	EA.	73.50	50.00	123.50
75w	"	77.00	50.00	127.00
100w	"	79.00	50.00	129.00
Light track single circuit				
2'	EA.	19.75	16.60	36.35
4'	"	36.80	16.60	53.40
8'	"	66.00	33.20	99.20
Fixtures, square				
R-20	EA.	52.50	4.80	57.30
R-30	"	55.00	4.80	59.80
Mini spot	"	72.50	4.80	77.30
16670.10 LIGHTNING PROTECTION				
Lightning protection				
Copper point, nickel plated, 12'				
1/2" dia.	EA.	25.40	33.20	58.60
5/8" dia.	"	30.00	33.20	63.20

RESISTANCE HEATING	UNIT	MAT.	INST.	TOTAL
16850.10 ELECTRIC HEATING				
Baseboard heater				
2', 375w	EA.	34.30	33.20	67.50
3', 500w	"	42.30	33.20	75.50
4', 750w	"	52.50	37.90	90.40
5', 935w	"	70.00	44.20	114.20
6', 1125w	"	78.00	53.00	131.00
7', 1310w	"	97.00	60.50	157.50
8', 1500w	"	109.00	66.50	175.50
9', 1680w	"	120.00	73.50	193.50
10', 1875w	"	125.00	76.00	201.00
Unit heater wall mounted				
1500w	EA.	160.00	53.00	213.00
Thermostat				
Integral	EA.	26.30	16.60	42.90

Special Bonus Software Offer

As A Buyer Of A Building News 1992 Costbook You Are Eligible To Receive
— AT NO COST! —

CONSTRUCTION ESTIMATOR

The Complete, Stand Alone, Easy-To-Use, Construction Estimating System

- This program provides the basic tools to develop accurate, comprehensive and organized cost estimates.
- The reliable cost data can be used to supplement your own records and provides a basis for accurate estimating.

- IBM Compatible — 5¼" diskette.
- Immediate on-screen access to data through "Look-up" windows. "Pull-down" menus.
- Easy to learn and master — very user-friendly.
- Different markups can be applied to each estimate.

Act NOW And Receive – FREE – An Electronic Database With Over 1,000 Lines Of Building News Costbook Data

---

Order Form

NAME
_____

COMPANY
_____

ADDRESS
_____

CITY, STATE, ZIP
_____

TELEPHONE
_____

Simply fill out this form, read and sign the statement below and send this complete page to our East Coast office:
Building News Bookstore
77 Wexford Street
Needham Heights, MA 02194

I purchased my 1992 Costbook at: _____

STORE   CITY,   STATE

If you have received the Bonus Software through our mail offering, there is no need to order another. You may copy and share the software and data with co-workers and associates.

Bonus Software Qualifications

The PC-ESTIMATOR™ is a software product developed, produced and distributed by CPR International, Inc., 3195 Adeline Street, Suite A, Berkeley, CA 94703, (415) 654-8338. The electronic cost data provided with the PC-ESTIMATOR is derived from the Building News 1992 Construction Costbooks.

CPR International has no affiliation with BNI Publications Inc. (Building News). All questions regarding the software should be directed to CPR International, Inc.

BNI Publications Inc., its authors and editors, do not warrant or guarantee the correctness of the data or information contained in the costbooks. BNI Publications Inc., and its authors and editors, do hereby disclaim any responsibility or liability in connection with the use of data in electronic or printed form published by BNI Publications Inc., or other information in the database or costbooks.

I have read and agree to the above information.

_____
NAME - PLEASE SIGN

_____
NAME - PLEASE PRINT